WALK THE DIG, WILLIE

Robert Auletta

BROADWAY PLAY PUBLISHING INC
224 E 62nd St, NY, NY 10065
www.broadwayplaypub.com
info@broadwayplaypub.com

WALK THE DOG, WILLIE
© Copyright 1985 Robert Auletta

All rights reserved. This work is fully protected under the copyright laws of the United States of America. No part of this publication may be photocopied, reproduced, stored in a retrieval system, or transmitted, in any form or by any means, electronic, mechanical, recording, or otherwise, without the prior permission of the publisher. Additional copies of this play are available from the publisher.

Written permission is required for live performance of any sort. This includes readings, cuttings, scenes, and excerpts. For amateur and stock performances, please contact Broadway Play Publishing Inc. For all other rights please contact the author c/o B P P I.

Cover art by Steve Mellor

First edition: October 1985
This edition: October 2017
I S B N: 978-0-88145-032-3

Book design: Marie Donovan
Typeface: Palatino & Baskerville set by L&F Technical Composition, Lakeland, FL.

WALK THE DOG, WILLIE is
For Jeni,
Because she's got the moves.

WALK THE DOG, WILLIE played at The Production Company in New York City from 13 March through 14 April 1985, with the following cast:

BIJOU BILLINS.......................... Larry Bryggman
JENNIFER .... Amy Steel
MR. BROWFIELD..................... Evan Thompson
AUNTIE ROSE BILLINS................. Lilene Mansell
LOU ANN BILCOT.......... Kathleen Mahoney-Bennett
RONNIE BILLINS......................... Dan Butler
WILLIE.................... William Converse-Roberts

The setting was by Mike Boak; costumes by Walker Hicklin; lighting by Debra J. Kletter; and sound by David Gotwald. Jack Doulin was the Production Stage Manager; Colette Brooks the Dramaturg; and Norman René the Director.

An earlier version of WALK THE DOG, WILLIE was produced at the Yale Repertory Theatre. It opened on 15 January 1976 and ran through 17 March, with the following cast:

BIJOU BILLINS........................... Tom Hill
JENNIFER...................... Christine Estabrook
MR. BROWFIELD................... Eugene Trobnick
AUNTIE ROSE BILLINS............... Norma Brustein
LOU ANN BILCOT..................... Lynn Oliver
RONNIE BILLINS...................... Chuck Levin
WILLIE................................. Ken Ryan

Walt Jones was the Director; Michael Yeargan designed the set.

INTRODUCTION

The first production of Robert Auletta's *Walk the Dog, Willie* was in 1976 at the Yale Repertory Theater. Sam Shepard's *Buried Child* was written in 1978 or 79. I'm not suggesting that because of the evident similarity of the two plays Shepard must have borrowed from Auletta or been influenced by him; I haven't any idea whether or not Shepard even knows that *Willie* exists. No, something more interesting is at work here: a cultural confluence, an affinity of consciousnesses, a resemblance of attitudes, most specifically a shared sense of the heartland American family as rooted in strains of madness and violence, simultaneously sustained and corrupted by myths and bound by a love that more than touches on despair.

Buried Child is well enough known for me not to have to do more than refer to it in this prefatory note. But *Walk the Dog, Willie* isn't nearly as well known as it ought to be. It's an extremely disturbing play, not just because of the horrific violence that erupts at the end but, much more subtly, because of the way it modulates (even more fluidly than does Shepard's drama) between violence and wit, lament and send-up. We like to keep our emotional and artistic categories separate and clean, but *Willie* doesn't permit this; "gallows humor" is the common descriptive for one such fusion of contrarieties, and Auletta's play brilliantly exemplifies this way of handling imaginatively our situation of having to laugh in order (as Ionesco once said) not to cry.

"This is an authentic American family," Ronnie, the strangely furious and damaged son, says without irony about the besieged, demented Billins clan. And again, just before he is stabbed to death, "I have to stay here ... forever with my loved ones."

Jennifer, the "artist" of the group, the writer in crisis who says of words that "they used to be my friends at school.

But then they started attacking me," had once, apparently while in a mental institution, written in her own blood on cardboard the words "Kill Me." "It's short, Jennifer," Browfield the family friend tells her. "It's to the point. It's got emotion." To which the father, Bijou Billins, adds: "A very promising early work."

We're constantly thrown off guard by such wit in the face of horror, Auletta's intention being, I think, to keep us from seeing the family as a case history, such as so many of our recent domestic dramas unfortunately do give us. The same strategy shows itself in the mysterious nature of the characters, who in their unaccountability are more nearly "true to life" than any genre of naturalism can achieve. This is especially true of Willie and Ronnie, whose injuries seem to go beyond social and even psychic data. No explanations; no trafficking with "causes." We don't know *who* they are. What we do end by knowing is their extreme condition, the incarnation in them of experiences within a realm from which we most often avert our glances.

RICHARD GILMAN

CHARACTERS

BIJOU BILLINS.................... Head of household
AUNTIE ROSE BILLINS..................... His wife
RONNIE BILLINS.......................... Their son
MR. BROWFIELD................. A friend of the family
LOU ANN BILCOT................. Ronnie's girlfriend
JENNIFER......................... Willie's girlfriend
WILLIE

Act One takes place in the backyard of an old white frame house. The house is not poverty stricken, but certainly needs work. There are some lawn furniture—chaise lounges, etc.—and a barbecue scattered about. A swing hangs from an old tree. The yard is surrounded by a cyclone-type fence.

Act Two takes place inside an animal hospital. There are cages with dogs in them, a couple of operating tables, a refrigerator, an old radio, a couple of stools, etc.

The play begins on a Saturday morning, about eleven o'clock. The time is the present. The place is somewhere in the Midwest.

(*Note*: See Prop List and Costume Plot at end of play.)

ACT ONE

(*It is Saturday morning. The lights come up on the back porch of the Billins' house. The sounds of birds are heard. We hear* JENNIFER'S *voice offstage.*)

JENNIFER: Willie! Willie!

(*She comes running onstage. Her hair is in a pony tail. She is wearing a dress and sneakers.*)

Willie! Ahh, come on, Willie. (*She kicks something*) Willie! Willie!

(*The door of the house opens.* BIJOU BILLINS *enters.*)

BILLINS: Hi, Jennifer.

JENNIFER: Hi, Mr. Billins.

BILLINS: Waiting for Willie?

JENNIFER: Did you see him?

BILLINS: I heard him early this morning, I think. But I haven't seen him since.

JENNIFER: He's supposed to meet me here at eleven.

BILLINS: It's just five after.

JENNIFER: My watch says twelve.

BILLINS: You're fast, Jennifer.

JENNIFER: (*Adjusting her watch*) About six after now?

BILLINS: You're right on target, Jennifer.

JENNIFER: (*Looking about*) I wonder...

BILLINS: He'll be here soon enough, I'll bet.

JENNIFER: (*Staring at* BILLINS) Hey, You look great, Mr. Billins. Is that a new shirt?

BILLINS: Sure is. Got it the other day at one of those two-for-one sales.

JENNIFER: It's great.

BILLINS: Well, thank you, Jennifer. (*He looks around, then stretches a bit.*) Ahh, what a day. (*Pause*) He's always late, isn't he?

JENNIFER: Yeah.

BILLINS: He never liked creamed spinach as a kid. He came late to the table because we were always having it. Always eating creamed spinach. (*Pause*) "I'll spite that spinach," he said. That fouled up stuff.

JENNIFER: What?

BILLINS: The creamed spinach.

JENNIFER: We never ate it.

BILLINS: But you liked it, I'll bet.

JENNIFER: When we ate it. I liked it. But we never had it.

BILLINS: "I'll spite those pork chops," he said. (*Pause*) You're a good girl.

JENNIFER: Yeah.

BILLINS: He was a good boy.

JENNIFER: Sure is.

BILLINS: He always walked the dog.

JENNIFER: You had a dog?

BILLINS: The old dog, Shep.

JENNIFER: Was he the sheep dog?

BILLINS: We called him Shep. But he wasn't a sheep dog.

JENNIFER: But the other dog, the one that came...

BILLINS: The sheep dog was Willie's original dog. She came with him.

JENNIFER: (*Softly*) She came with him.

BILLINS: What a dog. Never left his side ... till they say she choked to death ... on a turkey bone.

ACT ONE

JENNIFER: I didn't know about ... choking.

BILLINS: I thought Willie told you everything, Jennifer.

JENNIFER: (*Without looking at her watch.*) Do you have the time?

BILLINS: (*Without looking at his watch.*) Five after eleven.

JENNIFER: Thanks.

BILLINS: The only thing he ever loved, and choked to death on a turkey bone.

JENNIFER: Not the only!

BILLINS: Nearly the only.

JENNIFER: Not the only!

BILLINS: Almost the only.

JENNIFER: You gave her that turkey bone, didn't you, Mr. Billins? You shoved it into her mouth.

BILLINS: Now how are you going to prove that, Jennifer?

JENNIFER: I'll go back. I'll find out. I'll search.

BILLINS: Of course you will. But the only one who knows for sure is the dog; and the dog is dead. So, you see, Jennifer, we can never know for sure.

JENNIFER: Are you lying?

BILLINS: (*Some panic*) Did you make me lie?

JENNIFER: (*Looking around*) There's nobody else, there's nobody else here. Just you and I. Then I guess I did.

BILLINS: You sure did.

JENNIFER: I made you into a liar.

BILLINS: That's right, that's right. You made me into ... a low-life liar. That's what you did ... right here in my presence.

JENNIFER: I made you into what you are, a dirt-eating liar.

BILLINS: Nobody else.

JENNIFER: Nobody else would have wanted to make you into what you are: a mud-mouthing, scum-sucking liar.

BILLINS: Only you, Jennifer.

JENNIFER: Imagine that. Just me. (*Pause*) The dog is dead.

BILLINS: Just you and me.

JENNIFER: I thought you said, just me?

BILLINS: I meant to say, just you. I want to stand on what I say, Jennifer.

JENNIFER: You read my thoughts.

BILLINS: How do you mean?

JENNIFER: I want to stand on what I say, too. I said, Willie: I want to stand on what I say.

BILLINS: And then what did he do.

JENNIFER: He ripped my dress clean off, for starters.

BILLINS: That boy always had ... fast reflexes.

JENNIFER: He said I was a naked sky witch; wanted to see me that way, posed against the sky for him.

BILLINS: Jennifer, aaaaaa. ...

JENNIFER: It was a bad time for him. He was so close to it.

BILLINS: To what, Jennifer?

JENNIFER: Death, death! Don't you remember that?

BILLINS: Like it was yesterday.

JENNIFER: Was it yesterday, Mr. Billins?

BILLINS: Now let me see, Jennifer. (*He starts counting off on his fingers.*) It was ... (*Starts to chuckle*) Too long ago to be yesterday.

JENNIFER: Stop that!

BILLINS: What?

JENNIFER: You were about to laugh.

BILLINS: I'm not laughing.

JENNIFER: Your stupid face was about to laugh.

BILLINS: I'll never laugh, Jennifer. I'll kneel down and promise and swear...

JENNIFER: Willie!

BILLINS: What's up?

JENNIFER: Shut him up, Willie! (*She paces around.*) Shit. (*She kicks at something.*) He's stood me up.

BILLINS: I was kind of like a father to him. He was kind of like a little kid to me. He'd come running to me, I'd hoist him into the air, laughing merrily; then he'd cough right into my fucking face.

JENNIFER: Watch your language! Willie never spoke to me like that.

BILLINS: I'll just bet.

(JENNIFER *paces a bit more, then stops and looks at* BILLINS.)

JENNIFER: Are they new socks you've got on there, Mr. Billins?

BILLINS: No, they're an old pair. In fact, they're my oldest ones.

(*She paces, stops, looks around.*)

JENNIFER: He's probably sleeping out there somewhere. Down by the river, I'll bet.

BILLINS: (*Worried*) Well, anyway ... (*Pause*) You know, we could probably talk considerably about Willie, the two of us.

JENNIFER: (*Staring at him*) Yeah.

BILLINS: And if we did, you know what I'd say?

JENNIFER: You tell me, Mr. Billins.

BILLINS: Willie was all right as far as all right goes, but...

JENNIFER: What?

BILLINS: But he had one fault, minor though a major one:
(*Pause as* JENNIFER *stares at him.*)
He lacked perfection.
(JENNIFER *laughs.*)
That's the way I see it, anyway.
(*She laughs again.*)
You know, there are perfect ones, Jennifer, there really are.

JENNIFER: Willie and I hate your perfect ones, Mr. Billins.

BILLINS: Just the other day, at the A and W Rootbeer stand I spied a perfect one, the most perfect one I had seen in a long time. I was holding a chocolate shake.

JENNIFER: What did you do?

BILLINS: I laughed and started crying happy.

JENNIFER: What happened to your shake?

BILLINS: Well, I got so excited that I dropped it on my shoes.

JENNIFER: And your pants, too. Look at your pants.

BILLINS: I cleaned my shoes.

JENNIFER: But you didn't clean your fucking pants.

BILLINS: You'll pay for that, Jennifer.

JENNIFER: Your shit-slob pants, why don't you rinse 'em out?

BILLINS: Jennifer, Jennifer...

JENNIFER: Willie and I really hate your perfect ones, Mr. Billins; you see, they're not perfect at all; they're just like your pants. (*Pause*) I can't stand it anymore, Mr. Billins.

BILLINS: (*Frightened*) What?

JENNIFER: Unsnap my bra.

BILLINS: What? What?

ACT ONE

JENNIFER: Make believe you're Willie. Caress me. (*She starts moving toward him.*)

BILLINS: (*Moving away from her.*) Not me, not me. You'll just have to work things out on your own, Jennifer.

JENNIFER: Lick my tits.

BILLINS: Shut up! Shut up!

JENNIFER: Suzing my scuz.

BILLINS: I'll kill you.

JENNIFER: Itching my goo.

BILLINS: We're outside, Jennifer. In front of houses.

JENNIFER: Scrambling his fingers into my goo gap.

BILLINS: (*Cries out and stamps his foot violently.*) Do you still write short stories?!

(*She stares at him.*)
You know what I'm saying?

JENNIFER: Yeah.

BILLINS: Well, do you still...

JENNIFER: I write beginnings ... and endings.

BILLINS: You burn with a literary passion.

JENNIFER: I burn.

BILLINS: Your talent interests me.

JENNIFER: Don't shoot your mouth off unless you can do some good.

BILLINS: What do you mean?

JENNIFER: Make it happen for me. Get me an agent. Get me visible in a national known magazine.

BILLINS: I'm not promising anything.

JENNIFER: But are you willing to try?

BILLINS: I do have some connections.

JENNIFER: Who with, tramps and criminals?

BILLINS: Now listen, Jennifer, that's...

JENNIFER: (*Laughing*) I'm only kidding, Mr. Billins. You know me.

BILLINS: I certainly do.

JENNIFER: (*Getting agitated*) Well, I guess I better be going. It's no fun for a girl getting stood up, you know.

(BILLINS *just stares at her.*)

I'm fed up with life the way it is.

BILLINS: So are we all, Jennifer.

JENNIFER: Even dogs want it better.

BILLINS: They certainly do. But dogs know how to keep their place.

JENNIFER: What's my place, Mr. Billins?

BILLINS: Well, I imagine...

JENNIFER: (*Suddenly cries out heartbreakingly...*) Willie!

BILLINS: Quiet!

JENNIFER: Just testing to hear the echo.

BILLINS: There's never been no echo around here.

JENNIFER: Since time started ticking?

BILLINS: Well, that certainly was a long time ago.

JENNIFER: So what do you know, you fucking skiball.

BILLINS: I want to tell you something, Jennifer.

JENNIFER: I'm just ears.

BILLINS: I once knew an old man whose bowels didn't move for so long that he finally died. I don't mean to be vulgar.

JENNIFER: Did Willie know him?

BILLINS: Yes. He lived with us here for a while. At night I would go into his room and strike him across the face. Not at full strength, you understand.

ACT ONE

JENNIFER: Sure.

BILLINS: He was old, you see. But hard enough, hard enough. How do you like that, old man? Well, he was old. He hardly knew what was going on. It was all a furry, noisy blur to him, I think. He was better off than the rest of us.

JENNIFER: Sure.

BILLINS: Though once I think I broke his nose.

JENNIFER: Did he cry?

BILLINS: That time he did. The only time. I finally reached him. An amazing thing those tears. I was completely amazed.

JENNIFER: Willie'll get you for it, Billins.

BILLINS: (*Smiling*) Willie never knew.

JENNIFER: Of course he knew. Check again.

BILLINS: That's impossible to fulfill, Jennifer. In fact, most things you say are extreme in an impossible way, you understand.

JENNIFER: That's the way I am.

BILLINS: Then it's all settled.

JENNIFER: It certainly is.

BILLINS: Good. Because I'm going in and watch some TV.

JENNIFER: Lucky you.

BILLINS: I'm not going to say goodbye, Jennifer.

JENNIFER: Naturally that's fine with me.

(BILLINS *goes into the house.* JENNIFER *sits down on the steps and begins to stare into the distance. After a while she sees something. She starts to get excited. Strange music is heard. She is about to cry out. The music starts to fade. The vision blurs.* BILLINS *comes back out.*)

JENNIFER: Look.

BILLINS: What?

JENNIFER: Can't you see? Over there.

BILLINS: (*Squinting*) Can't see.

JENNIFER: Make your hands into binoculars. Like this.

(*She makes her hands into binoculars. He does the same.*)

BILLINS: I can see now.

JENNIFER: Sure. Look. It's a crowd of people. They're lifting a ... young man on top of their shoulders. They're cheering him.

BILLINS: Wow.

JENNIFER: And there's a band. Hear the band?

BILLINS: Sure.

JENNIFER: And fireworks. See the fireworks?

BILLINS: Sure.

JENNIFER: And it's getting more and more ... so beautiful, I can't describe it. Can you?

BILLINS: It's too beautiful. It's ... (*Suddenly* BILLINS *jumps to his feet and rushes into the house. We hear him cry out as he smashes something.*)

(*The music and the vision begin to disappear.*)

JENNIFER: You ruined it! You ruined! You ruined it, you fucking skiball! (*Crying out*) Willie! Willie!

(*Silence, and then* BILLINS *comes back out. He seems very composed. She pays no attention to him.*)

BILLINS: Any chance you've seen a newspaper lying around? (*He pokes around a bit.*) That does it. I'm cancelling my subscription.

JENNIFER: (*Pathetically*) I want a Dr. Pepper.

BILLINS: There's no more Dr. Pepper.

JENNIFER: What'll I do?

BILLINS: Drink battery acid.

JENNIFER: What'll I do! What'll I do?

ACT ONE

BILLINS: F-I-L-T-H. You get it, Jennifer?

(*She stares at him.*)

That's all there is. The sum total. I'm talking about history and all its people. (*Pause*) A wife killed her husband with a pitchfork, while he was saying his prayers.

JENNIFER: No.

BILLINS: It was always like that. Even when I was a little boy. Once I woke up and found a whole field covered with dead birds.

JENNIFER: No. Flying.

BILLINS: They weren't flying. Not when I found them. They were grounded, Jennifer. They were earthed.

JENNIFER: (*Looking around*) I want, I want...

BILLINS: We're all out of it, Miss. It's all ruined.

(*She moans a bit and begins to withdraw into herself, rocking back and forth a bit.*)

That's the ticket. That's the way to town, all right.

(BROWFIELD *enters. He is dressed, as usual, in a natty fashion.*)

BROWFIELD: Hey, Bijou, how you doing?

BILLINS: Oh, I'm looking up, Brow, looking up.

BROWFIELD: That's the ticket. And there's sweet honeysuckle. What are you doing, waiting for Willie as usual?

(*She pays no attention to him.*)

I'm talking to you, honey pie.

JENNIFER: Yup.

BROWFIELD: Can't you keep that boy in line, Bijou?

BILLINS: Oh, he comes and goes.

BROWFIELD: Ain't it the way with the young. (*Going over to* JENNIFER.) How's those stories coming, sugar cat?

JENNIFER: (*Coming out of it a bit.*) I'm improving. My style's improving.

BROWFIELD: Hot dog.

JENNIFER: My words are improving. My words make sense.

BROWFIELD: That's the best policy.

JENNIFER: I mean, you know me for a long time. You've known me for years and years.

BROWFIELD: Oh, that I have, lambchop, that I have.

BILLINS: Funny, I thought you two just met. (*He laughs.*)

BROWFIELD: Cram it up, Bijou.

JENNIFER: You knew me when my words didn't make sense.

BROWFIELD: Like it was yesterday.

JENNIFER: It may have been yesterday, Mr. Browfield. I don't really know. Was it yesterday?

BROWFIELD: Take my word for it, it wasn't. It just seems that way.

JENNIFER: I couldn't handle them, you know, those meanings of words.

BROWFIELD: I remember, Jennifer.

JENNIFER: (*Starting to get crazy.*) Those buzzing, buzzings. ... They used to be my friends in school. But then they started attacking me.

BROWFIELD: Ahh, school! School days, dear old Golden Rule days! Right, Bijou?

BILLINS: Those were the days.

BROWFIELD: The formation of character. (*To* JENNIFER) Bijou and I went completely through education together.

BILLINS: The way we used to write the answers on our hands before examinations.

ACT ONE

BROWFIELD: Just a little cheating.

JENNIFER: Willie would know.

BROWFIELD: What's that, Jennifer?

JENNIFER: How to make the words stop attacking me.

BROWFIELD: I'm not sure if he would, Jennifer.

BILLINS: Another one of her stupid ideas, Brow. She's got a million of 'em.

JENNIFER: (*Getting frantic*) Willie would know!

BILLINS: Listen here, Jennifer...

JENNIFER: But he took this long trip, packed his bags...

BROWFIELD: Ahh, that's a sad story, Jennifer.

JENNIFER: Got lost in the moon books, in the pigeon eyes of the night...

BILLINS: Pigeon eyes.

JENNIFER: It's then I started getting funny.

BILLINS: You were always funny.

JENNIFER: No. I can prove it. Because it was then my speech started getting haywire; my speech started going: aaa gaaa.

BILLINS: I don't remember that.

JENNIFER: Sure it did. It started going: (*Gaining in volume and force*) aaaa gaaaa.

BROWFIELD: Sure she did, Bijou. Just like that.

BILLINS: I don't remember.

JENNIFER: Just like now. (*Pursuing* BILLINS) Aaaaa gaaaaa, aaaaa gaaaa. (*Her voice grows in violence and intensity as* BILLINS *tries to escape her.*) Aaaaaaaa gaaaaaa, aaaaaaa gaaaaaaa, aaaaaaa gaaaaaaa.

BILLINS: Shut her up, Brow! Shut her up!

JENNIFER: AAAAAAAAAAAAAA GAAAAAAAAAAAAA.

BILLINS: Brow!

BROWFIELD: Ahh, she's just letting off a little steam, Bijou.

JENNIFER: (*Staring at* BILLINS, *calmly.*) Blood.

BILLINS: She's on the loose again, Brow.

BROWFIELD: I think you're overreacting a bit, Bijou.

BILLINS: Bring her to a standstill, Brow. You know how. You're the man for the job.

JENNIFER: (*Softly*) Blood.

BROWFIELD: All she needs is a little understanding. (*He puts his arm around her.*) A little delicacy in handling. (*He begins caressing her sensuously.*) Isn't that right, honeysuck? Haven't I always been extremely delicate in my handling of you? (*Beat*) Let us escort you down memory lane.

BILLINS: Like we once escorted you to the lunatic asylum.

JENNIFER: No. (*Her body goes rigid.*) Never been there.

BROWFIELD: Looney city, Jennifer. Don't you remember the sights?

JENNIFER: Never once ever there.

BILLINS: Don't shit us, Jennifer.

JENNIFER: Not even in a dream. (*She rushes over to the swing, gets on it, and begins swinging back and forth.*) You're thinking of some other pretty girl.

(BILLINS *walks over to her.*)

BILLINS: I'm going to refresh your memory.

BROWFIELD: (*Going over*) You know, Bijou, it might be better ... not to refresh her any more than we already have.

BILLINS: But, Brow, it's Willie.

BROWFIELD: What about Willie?

BILLINS: It's to get him out of these precincts, to get him out of her head—that's why I want to refresh her good.

(BROWFIELD *just stares at him.*)

Do you follow my drift, Brow?

BROWFIELD: I follow your drift, Bijou.

BILLINS: I mean, we were always honest men.

BROWFIELD: Known for it. Throughout the county.

(*The men laugh.* BROWFIELD *begins pushing the swing.*)

JENNIFER: I never been in nobody's nut house.

BROWFIELD: Isn't she cute?

BILLINS: I don't think so. In fact, I think she's a tramp, Brow.

BROWFIELD: Ahh, come on, Bijou. Come down off your high horse.

JENNIFER: Never been, never been there.

BILLINS: You were the poet in residence.

JENNIFER: I don't write poems.

BILLINS: I've been told by people in charge that you wrote filthy poems in the nut house.

JENNIFER: I never wrote no filthy poems in nobody's nut house.

BROWFIELD: You know, I've got over two hundred thousand dollars in the bank, Jennifer, and do you know how I got it? By remembering things, Jennifer, by remembering important things.

JENNIFER: Right on the money.

(BROWFIELD *laughs.*)

BILLINS: We'll go down to the newspapers, Brow, get the clippings, the clippings that detail her activities that sent her to the nut house. Make her read 'em.

(*The men laugh.*)

JENNIFER: You boys are pigs. 'Cept pigs are better.

(*The men laugh.*)

BROWFIELD: You know what the problem is, Bijou?

BILLINS: What's that, Brow?

BROWFIELD: We never grew up!

BILLINS: Ain't it the truth!

BROWFIELD: And thank God, I say.

(*The men laugh.*)

JENNIFER: 'Cause pigs are better as people.

(*The men laugh.*)

BROWFIELD: You know what I've been told, Bijou?

BILLINS: What's that, Brow?

BROWFIELD: That sometimes it gets rocky in the nuthouse. That sometimes the nuts get jolted around. (*He begins to push the swing wildly about.*) Sometimes it gets real rough in there.

(JENNIFER *cries out.*)

BILLINS: Sock it to her, Brow! Sock it to her!

(JENNIFER *tries to get off the swing, but instead she falls. The men stand there, watching her.*)

BROWFIELD: Can we give you a hand, sweetheart?

JENNIFER: No.

BROWFIELD: Ahh, come on. (*He starts going to her.*)

(JENNIFER *gets up.*)

JENNIFER: Willie'll come and squeeze the fire right out of your faces!

(*The men laugh.*)

Burn your eyes!

BILLINS: Hey, I've got an idea, Brow.

ACT ONE

BROWFIELD: What is it, Bijou?

BILLINS: A peach of an idea, Brow.

BROWFIELD: Then go to it, Bijou.

(BILLINS *goes into the house.* JENNIFER *begins wandering aimlessly about, talking a bit to herself.*)

BROWFIELD: That Bijou's a ball of fire.

JENNIFER: Were you talking to me, sir?

BROWFIELD: (*Staring at her*) Ahh, yes. I was.

JENNIFER: Good. Because I wanted to ask you a question.

BROWFIELD: I'm at your service.

JENNIFER: You see, I'm having a lot of problems.

BROWFIELD: Whereabouts? (*Smiling*) In the pelvic area ... or the head area?

JENNIFER: Moreabouts the head area.

BROWFIELD: (*Stifling a laugh*) Oh, that's too bad.

JENNIFER: You see, I'm having a lot of trouble with characters, Mr. Browfield.

BROWFIELD: What seems to be the problem.

JENNIFER: They don't seem to exist anymore. I can't find them out there.

BROWFIELD: Oh, they're out there all right. Just keep looking.

JENNIFER: I don't think so, Mr. Browfield.

BROWFIELD: What about your punctuation? Have you been working on your sloppy punctuation, Jennifer?

JENNIFER: Not as much as I should, I'm afraid.

BROWFIELD: Well, forget about characters, Jennifer. And go home and work on that grungey punctuation of yours.

JENNIFER: I know you speak on my behalf, Mr. Browfield.

BROWFIELD: Without a doubt.

JENNIFER: But what is a character, Mr. Browfield, a living, real character?

BROWFIELD: A man with clothes. Nice clothes.

JENNIFER: Oh.

BROWFIELD: And money in his pocket.

JENNIFER: Is that all?

BROWFIELD: That's it.

(BILLINS *enters. He is holding a piece of cardboard in his hand.*)

BILLINS: A little momento from her institutional stay. (*He holds up a cardboard. Scrawled on it with blood are the words: Kill Me.*) Direct from the looney bin, this masterpiece. (*He grins.*)

JENNIFER: (*Begins to tremble*) I didn't write it.

BROWFIELD: It's short, Jennifer. It's to the point. It has emotion.

BILLINS: A very promising early work.

JENNIFER: I know who did it. But I can't tell.

BROWFIELD: Be proud, Jen, be proud.

JENNIFER: I couldn't work there. I need Willie around to do my work.

BROWFIELD: A true writer writes.

JENNIFER: They attacked him and drove him away.

BROWFIELD: A true writer writes in blood.

JENNIFER: They hurt him. They hurt me.

BILLINS: I'm crazy about this. I'm gonna have it framed.

BROWFIELD: A true writer writes useless things in blood. You gotta expect people to laugh.

(*The men laugh uproariously.*)

JENNIFER: No.

BILLINS: She refuses to own up, Brow. Look at it Jennifer.

(*She turns away from it.*)

JENNIFER: No!

BILLINS: Look at it, look at it. (*He starts pursuing her frantically, trying to shove the cardboard in her face.*) Your blood, your prints.

BROWFIELD: Bijou, don't you think it would be better if you. ...

BILLINS: I'm sick and tired of her rebelliousness, Brow. It goes against my grain.

BROWFIELD: Ok, then do what you want.

(*He starts pursuing her. She tries to evade him.*)

BILLINS: Your blood, your prints. Your blood, your prints, (*etc.*).

(JENNIFER *cries out and sinks to the ground, withdrawing totally into herself.*)

BROWFIELD: Look at this.

JENNIFER: (*She begins rocking back and forth saying over and over:*)
Oh, Willie and I,
Willie no more.

BROWFIELD: Look what we're saddled with now.

BILLINS: She asked for it, Brow.

BROWFIELD: You know, sometimes I think you're a fucking moron, Bijou.

BILLINS: You shouldn't say that, Browfield.

BROWFIELD: Why's that?

BILLINS: Because she's the one you should be dead set against. She's the actual one.

BROWFIELD: Who knows? Maybe you're right.

BILLINS: I've thought about it a long time. (*Pause*) I've thought and thought about it.

(*The sounds of birds.* BILLINS *stares up into the air.* BROWFIELD *stands there thinking.* JENNIFER *is now silent and unmoving. Suddenly the door opens and* AUNTIE ROSE *enters. She is carrying a pitcher of lemonade.*)

ROSE: Lemonade, boys and girls! Lemonade!

BILLINS: Great idea, Rose.

BROWFIELD: You've read my mind once more, Rose.

(*They walk over to the porch and sit down.*)

ROSE: Be back in a jiffy. (*She goes back into the house.*)

BILLINS: What times we used to have, Brow. What times.

BROWFIELD: We still do, Bijou. We still have a way with it all.

BILLINS: Ain't it the truth, Brow.

(JENNIFER *makes a sharp little sound. They glance at her.*)

(*Now* ROSE *enters, carrying glasses.*)

ROSE: Glasses, boys and girls! Glasses!

BILLINS: Oh, boy.

(ROSE *fills the glasses and passes them around.*)

ROSE: Yoo hoo, Jennifer. Want some lemonade?

BILLINS: She's not thirsty.

ROSE: Pity.

BILLINS: (*Staring at his glass.*) Ahhh.

(*Now they all drink.*)

BROWFIELD: Mmmmmmm, mmmmmmm. Rosey does it again.

ROSE: Fresh lemons and lots of sugar!

BROWFIELD: Yummy delisch.

BILLINS: Very delisch, Rose.

ACT ONE

BROWFIELD: By the way, Rose, is that a new smock you're wearing?

ROSE: Oh, you can't mean this poor old thing.

BROWFIELD: Oh, Rose, it's a little stunner and you know it.

(ROSE *giggles*.)

She knows it, doesn't she, Bijou.

BILLINS: She sure knows it.

ROSE: (*Coyly*) L'il 'ol me?

BROWFIELD: Rose, let me tell you: You really know it.

BILLINS: (*Staring at his glass*) Ahhhhh.

ROSE: By the way, Willie was just here.

(JENNIFER *stands up*.)

JENNIFER: Where?

BILLINS: Take a walk, Jennifer.

ROSE: In the back room. But he's gone now.

BILLINS: Come on, Rose. Have some more lemonade.

ROSE: Dropped in unexpectedly, he did. I didn't have any time to prepare.

BROWFIELD: No use paying any attention to that kind of unexpected visit, Rose. Best thing to do is just put it out of your mind.

BILLINS: Just stick it right out of your mind.

ROSE: Just standing there. As big as life. Not so much as a how-do-you-do.

BILLINS: Ease off, Rose.

JENNIFER: Why didn't you call me?

ROSE: I almost screamed. (*Softly*) Willie, Willie.

BILLINS: (*Softly*) She's been quiet for a long time up until now, Brow.

ROSE: So I picked up the porcelain tray and offered him a brownie. As a friendly gesture, you understand.

BILLINS: Rose makes fantastic brownies.

ROSE: So he held a brownie in his hand. Just started at it. It seemed a long time. Don't you like my cooking, Willie? Don't you like my home-baked specialties?

BILLINS: He's a fool if he doesn't, Rose.

ROSE: And then he dropped it on the floor. And ground it up with his foot.

(JENNIFER *tries to race into the house.*)

JENNIFER: I want to see the crumbs!

(BROWFIELD *grabs her.*)

BILLINS: She'll try and eat 'em, Brow.

JENNIFER: (*Struggling*) No. I just want to put them in my pocket.

ROSE: But I wasn't about to be bullied by him. That's not my style.

BILLINS: That's not your style, Rose.

ROSE: I know what my style is. (*Pause*) Willie, I said, since you have returned back to the home, you will now behave as other members of this family are trained to behave. Since in your own peculiar way you were once ... (*Drifting now*) membered, membering, remembered of the family members, membered, memberless ... Willie...

BILLINS: How about a nice nap, Rose?

(*She goes over to the swing. There is a strange smile on her face.*)

ROSE: The only thing to do was to talk sense to him.

BILLINS: Rose is dollars and cents all the way.

ROSE: (*Offhand*) Shut up.

ACT ONE

BILLINS: Right, Rose.

(She gets on the swing and starts swinging back and forth, very coquettishly. She is humming something now. Suddenly she stops swinging.)

ROSE: Chores! This family is based on the principle that there are at least always a million chores to do. So now, Willie, I've got a chore for you to do. There's your old dog, Shep. Remember him? Now listen carefully, Willie. And obey me strictly. I want you to walk the dog, Willie. Walk him, Willie. Now don't give me any back talk or try to get out of it in any spiteful way. Now here's the leash. Now walk him, Willie. Walk Shep, Willie. (*The life seems to go out of her. She starts swinging slowly.*)

BILLINS: I'll bet he didn't. Willie was never good with chores.

BROWFIELD: You asshole.

BILLINS: Huh?

(She stops swinging.)

ROSE: So he moved slowly towards his old friend. And they're smelling each other. Smelling the life out of each other. And their eyes are glowing. Shep's blind eyes. And Willie's almost ... living eyes.

BILLINS: How'd you stand it, Rose?

(She gets off the swing.)

ROSE: God was on my side!

BILLINS: Oh, He always is.

ROSE: Whenever Willie gets too close, Jesus comes into my heart.

JENNIFER: Oh, Jesus, Jesus.

BILLINS: Jesus is her ace in the hole.

ROSE: Then they started making these sounds: dreadful mutterings, spit sounds, little animal cries.

BROWFIELD: A truly awful business.

ROSE: I knew I couldn't stay there very long. I could feel my hair going white.

BILLINS: And you have such beautiful hair.

ROSE: I couldn't speak.

BROWFIELD: That boy Willie can rob you of the power to vocalize.

ROSE: But the plates!

BILLINS: The plates could speak?

ROSE: No. My pewter plates. My beautiful plates for the Centennial. His sounds grew so awful high and scary that he split three of them in half.

BROWFIELD: (*Shaking his head*) What a homecoming.

ROSE: And then...

BILLINS: Worse?

ROSE: Yes. At first there were two of them! Willie and Shep. But then they ... sort of ... they became one. Breathing and moving all around me.

BILLINS: Oh, Rose.

ROSE: It was then that I called Jesus!

BILLINS: From out of your heart!

ROSE: From out of my heart where He always is!

BILLINS: He likes it here!

ROSE: Sig him, Jesus! Sig him!

BROWFIELD: Get his ass, Jesus!

JENNIFER: (*Moving erratically about the stage.*) Run, Willie! Run!

ROSE: You should have seen it! Sig him, Jesus!

BROWFIELD: He get him, Rose?

ACT ONE

ROSE: Tore him to pieces!

BROWFIELD: Whooped his ass good!

BILLINS: Slammed him from here to hallelujah!

ROSE: A regular, down-to-Earth, hearth and home-protecting miracle!

BILLINS: Right.

ROSE: The Savior.

BILLINS: Who loves you a lot, Rose.

ROSE: Definitely.

BROWFIELD: If he goes to bat for her like that He must love her to pieces.

BILLINS: Right.

JENNIFER: Jesus is a stupid ape who comes from another planet.

ROSE: Don't make fun of the Lord our God!

JENNIFER: The who, our what? The who, our what?

ROSE: Haven't you ever been to Sunday School, young lady?

JENNIFER: Willie can beat Him. Willie can beat Him good. (*She goes over and sits on the swing and begins swinging slowly.*)

ROSE: How about some more lemonade?

BROWFIELD: That's the ticket, Rose.

(ROSE *fills the glasses. A kind of toast.*)

ROSE: Well, it always turns out right in the end.

BROWFIELD: Because people *in* the *right* can never be *too* *righteous*.

BILLINS: Right.

ROSE: That's life.

(*They drink. Now they put their glasses down and begin to drift off into a kind of nothingness.*)

BILLINS: Just look at that great big bluejay up there.

ROSE: He's got a peanut.

(*Back into nothingness. Only the sound of the swing is heard. After a few moments we hear a woman's scream coming from the house.*)

BROWFIELD: What?

(*Now we hear* RONNIE'S *voice coming from within the house.*)

RONNIE: (*Voice*) All right, you!

(*The woman screams again, and something goes crashing.*)

BILLINS: Burglars!

BROWFIELD: Think not.

BILLINS: What?

BROWFIELD: It's Ronnie.

BILLINS: Ronnie's away at school.

(*Another crash from within the house.*)

RONNIE: (*Voice*) C'mere, you hot little molecule. I wantta use you for a science experiment.

WOMAN: (*Voice*) Oh, no you don't! (*She screeches.*)

(*Sounds of pursuit*)

BROWFIELD: Whoever that burglar is he's doing a great imitation of Ronnie.

BILLINS: I just don't understand it.

BROWFIELD: He must be home on break, Bijou.

(*Sounds of moaning and erotic groaning*)

(*They all sit there, listening.*)

ROSE: He's a frisky one, isn't he?

BROWFIELD: He certainly is.

ACT ONE 27

RONNIE: (*Voice*) Now let's go and meet the folks.

WOMAN: Ronnie, nooooooo!

(RONNIE *comes running down the stairs and out onto the front porch. He is pulling* LOU ANN *by the arm. He is wearing dungarees and a shirt. His feet are bare.* LOU ANN *is wearing only a football jersey, and is squirming like mad, trying to get away.*)

LOU ANN: Hey, Ronnie. C'mon, Ronnie. Pleeeeaaasssssse.

BROWFIELD: Heyyyy, lookee, lookee.

BILLINS: When did you get home, Son?

RONNIE: It's the Ronnie and Lou Ann show!

ROSE: Ronnie goes to the State University. He's studying to be a veterinarian.

BILLINS: We know that, Rose.

ROSE: He's my son.

BILLINS: We know that too, Rose.

RONNIE: For our next trick, Ronnie is going to make Lou Ann's jersey levitate. (*He grabs the jersey.*)

LOU ANN: (*Fighting him*) No, Ronnie. Stop it! (*To the folks*) Hi, I'm Lou Ann.

RONNIE: She knows her name. Some of us had our doubts, but she comes across with her name. How about that, folks?

(BROWFIELD *claps.*)

Now tell them you last name and you'll get a prize.

LOU ANN: Bilcot.

RONNIE: How about that, folks! Her name is Bilcot!

(BROWFIELD *applauds.* RONNIE *pulls her close to him.*)

RONNIE: Now do you want your big prize, Lou Ann?

LOU ANN: (*Struggling*) Ronnnnniiiieeee. (*To the folks*) Hi.

RONNIE: Ok, we'll save her big prize for later. (*He lets go of her.*)

BROWFIELD: Been taking a break after your exams, have you, Ronnie?

RONNIE: They take a lot out of you.

ROSE: He's a frisky one, isn't he?

BROWFIELD: He certainly is.

RONNIE: Let me do the honors. It seems I've been lapse with the honors. Haven't I, gang?

BILLINS: Right.

RONNIE: You've all met Ms. Bilcot, haven't you?

ROSE: She's a dear.

RONNIE: Now Ms. Bilcot, I'd like you to meet my mother and father, two down-home body types from Hometown City, U.S.A.

BILLINS: That's us.

RONNIE: And ... Mr. Browfield, an honorary uncle, and a man of...

BROWFIELD: Honor.

RONNIE: Extreme honor, you might say. In fact, he's brought new meaning to the word. And over there, a true angel of brightness, a unique person, a family confidante from way back, our one and only singing, dancing, Jennifer.

LOU ANN: Hi.

JENNIFER: Do you sleep a lot in bed with Willie's brother Ronnie?

LOU ANN: Ahhhhh.

RONNIE: What a wacky and wonderful group. Don't you agree, Lou Ann?

LOU ANN: Yes. Yes, I do.

JENNIFER: Because if you do that makes you very important in my book.

RONNIE: (*Stage whisper*) She's obsessed with this Willie character.

BILLINS: Well, well, well we're all here.

JENNIFER: Except Willie.

BILLINS: Can it, Jennifer.

JENNIFER: But he was here, just a few minutes ago. Too bad you were sleeping, Ronnie.

RONNIE: (*Staring at her*) What was he doing here?

JENNIFER: He came over to visit your mother.

ROSE: Oh, he just popped by for a few moments.

RONNIE: And how was he?

JENNIFER: He was great. He knocked the shit out of Jesus, and scared the piss out of Auntie Rose.

ROSE: Come here, young lady! I want to talk to you.

JENNIFER: Nope.

RONNIE: (*On the edge*) It seems like I've got a bad habit of missing things. You see, this morning if I wasn't so obsessed, you know, scientifically obsessed with my friend Lou Ann here, I might have had a chance of a ... catching a glimpse of Willie.

ROSE: It's for the best, Ronnie.

RONNIE: I don't know. I don't know what's "best" anymore. What about you, Lou Ann?

LOU ANN: I pass.

RONNIE: But still ... (*Taking her arm*) I still think missing Willie is a real miss, a loss, striko ... because of you. (*He starts squeezing her arm.*)

LOU ANN: (*Wincing*) Ronnie!

RONNIE: What's 'a matter? I'm just kind of hugging your arm a bit with my fingers.

BROWFIELD: RONNie!

RONNIE: (*Letting go of her arm, angry.*) I'm talking to my girlfriend, Browfield.

BROWFIELD: Well, why don't you learn to speak in a gentler manner?

RONNIE: Ahh, Browfield, do you know what the problem is?

BROWFIELD: You tell me, Ronnie.

RONNIE: There's a split between you folks and us University kids. You just don't understand our signals.

BROWFIELD: Is that right?

RONNIE: Town and gown. You ever hear of it?

BROWFIELD: I've heard of it.

BILLINS: I've never heard of it.

RONNIE: Let me tell you about it: It's a ragged, bloody, awful split.

BILLINS: Is there no way to fix it up?

RONNIE: No, there isn't.

BROWFIELD: So how is life at the University, Ronnie?

RONNIE: There is a world there which I partake of—fully.

BROWFIELD: That's the ticket.

RONNIE: To the core.

ROSE: That's wonderful, isn't it? (*Pause*) He's my son, isn't he?

BILLINS: He definitely is.

RONNIE: Right to the core, Browfield.

BROWFIELD: You've never been one ... to deny yourself ... very much, have you, Ronnie?

RONNIE: I'm always in the thick of it, Browfield—because I'm haunted.

ACT ONE

BROWFIELD: (*Uneasy*) Oh. (*Pause*) What exactly is it, Ronnie ... haunts you?

RONNIE: It's just a feeling, Browfield.

BROWFIELD: Is it?

RONNIE: The feeling that I've missed something special, something extraordinary, and I'll never be able to find it again.

LOU ANN: (*Smiling*) Sometimes he goes on and on about stuff like this.

(RONNIE *shoots her a dirty look.*)

RONNIE: So to compensate for the loss I often glut myself on the core, even when the core would be best left alone, even when the core is contaminated. You get me, Browfield?

BROWFIELD: Yes, I do.

RONNIE: And then I make myself sick. Boy, do I make myself sick.

LOU ANN: He hasn't been in the greatest shape lately.

RONNIE: (*Smiling*) Why don't you shut your pretty mouth, Lou Ann?

LOU ANN: Listen, Ronnie, don't treat me like an idiot.

RONNIE: So you want to tell them about me? Well, go ahead. Tell them.

LOU ANN: They are your family, aren't they?

RONNIE: Nobody else's, baby.

LOU ANN: (*To the others*) Oh, it's no big deal. He just seems kind of sleepless lately—very disturbed.

ROSE: What is it, Son?

RONNIE: Malaise, deep malaise.

ROSE: (*To* BIJOU) What's that, in the malaria family?

BILLINS: It certainly sounds like it is.

RONNIE: So ... (*With an exuberent laugh*) I mean, who cares? Why let it get you down?

BROWFIELD: That's showing 'em, Ronnie!

RONNIE: I mean, that's life. And life can be lifeless, or life denying, or at the same time life-denying lifelessness, or in a similar way you can be a lifer, just a lifer locked in to some kind of wall, prison wall ... What do you think, Browfield?

BROWFIELD: (*Staring at him*) I think you may be right, Ronnie.

RONNIE: Do you remember World War Two, Browfield?

BROWFIELD: Our finest hour.

RONNIE: The Pacific action, to nail it down?

BROWFIELD: Sure.

RONNIE: Well, there was a lot of savagery on those islands, you know. Sometimes the Americans would trap a group of Japanese down in their bunkers or tunnels, and instead of spending a little time trying to talk them out, getting someone who spoke Japanese or something, instead they would just get these flame throwers and pump fire down there into the darkness onto those screaming ... those roasting Japanese ... human bodies.

BROWFIELD: That's war.

RONNIE: It's an analogy, Browfield.

BROWFIELD: I get it.

ROSE: (*To* BILLINS) What are they talking about?

BILLINS: College talk.

RONNIE: So I wonder if they suffered from a problem similar to mine?

BROWFIELD: Who's that, Ronnie?

RONNIE: The fire pumpers, that's who.

BROWFIELD: Ahh haaa.

Act One

RONNIE: I wonder if after they were released from those islands, when they went back did they glut themselves out, sicken themselves out on the contaminated core?

BROWFIELD: What do you think, Bijou?

(BIJOU *shakes his head.*)

As far as I can guess I figure there's only one major Japanese problem those soldiers ever had to face.

BILLINS: What's that, Brow?

BROWFIELD: They can't go into a Jap restaurant without breaking out in hives!

(*The men laugh.*)

BILLINS: Did you get that, Rose?

ROSE: No.

BILLINS: It was funny.

ROSE: It was only an analogy, Browfield. A very strained analogy.

JENNIFER: Don't worry, Ronnie.

RONNIE: What, Jennifer?

JENNIFER: Willie will help you with your analogies.

RONNIE: Do you have much contact with Willie, Jennifer?

JENNIFER: Yes and no.

RONNIE: Well, the next time you have contact with him I want you to tell him something for me. Okay?

JENNIFER: Okay, Ronnie.

RONNIE: You be sure and tell him, if he ever comes around here again—I'm gonna rip his goddamn balls off!

JENNIFER: No, Ronnie.

BROWFIELD: Hey, Ronnie!

RONNIE: Hey, Browfield!

JENNIFER: You shouldn't say that, Ronnie. (*She begins to cry.*)

ROSE: I'm gonna rip 'em off and shove 'em down his throat!

JENNIFER: Willie will forgive you, Ronnie.

BILLINS: I think you ought to go in the house, Rose.

LOU ANN: You're a bastard, Ronnie.

RONNIE: You on me too, huh?

JENNIFER: Everything's going to be okay, Ronnie.

RONNIE: Nothing, nothing will ever be okay! Nothing!

BILLINS: Go into the house, Rose.

ROSE: Not while my son needs me.

RONNIE: Nothing!

(RONNIE *punches the side of the house with all his might.*)

Oh, shit. (*He sits down, holding his hand.*) Shit, shit, shit, shit.

ROSE: Oh, Ronnie, I'll go and get some ice cubes to put on it. (*She goes into the house.*)

(*Everybody just sits there for a while. The sound of birds is heard.*)

BILLINS: What do you study at the State University, Lou Ann?

LOU ANN: I'm not studying anything right now.

BILLINS: You all finished up?

LOU ANN: No, I just kind of ... stopped.

BILLINS: Oh. (*Pause*) What did you study when you were studying, Lou Ann?

LOU ANN: (*Thinking for a moment*) I forget.

BILLINS: Oh. (*Pause*) That's nice.

(*The sound of birds.*)

ACT ONE

(ROSE *enters.*)

ROSE: No more ice cubes, boys and girls.

BILLINS: You must have used them up all in the lemonade, Rose.

ROSE: No more ice cubes.

(*Everybody just sits there.*)

BILLINS: (*Stretching*) Aaaaaaaaaa. (*Pause*) Hey, I've got an idea. (*He gets up and goes into the house.*)

ROSE: Sometimes I just don't know what to do with that man.

BROWFIELD: One idea after another.

ROSE: I just can't contain him.

BROWFIELD: A regular ball of fire that Bijou.

(BILLINS *enters. He is carrying another piece of cardboard.*)

BILLINS: This is one of my favorites. (*He holds it up. Scrawled on it in blood are the words: Hurt Me Bad.*)

JENNIFER: (*Beginning to tremble*) It's a forgery.

(BILLINS *and* BROWFIELD *laugh.*)

ROSE: Now, now, boys, the girl made an honest attempt at her expression. No need to carry on so. (*She snickers.*)

BILLINS: Own up, Jennifer.

JENNIFER: They used my blood. But I didn't write it.

BROWFIELD: She's starting to use more complex sentences.

JENNIFER: They forced me. And took my blood. And wrote me. But I didn't write it.

(BILLINS *and* BROWFIELD *laugh.*)

BILLINS: Own up, Jennifer.

JENNIFER: Noooooooooo. (*She sinks to the ground, and then suddenly sees something there.*) Look at him lying there.

ROSE: Where?

BILLINS: Easy, Rose.

JENNIFER: The weather running out of his body. Blood moon from his chest. Stars exploding out of his head. Snow blowing out of his bones.

ROSE: (*Getting a grip on herself*) What a silly thing she is.

JENNIFER: I tried to hold him, but the wind took his living life like a kite.

(*Silence.*)

RONNIE: (*To* BILLINS) Can I see that for a minute?

BILLINS: Sure you can, Ronnie. (*He hands him the piece of cardboard.*)

RONNIE: Thanks. (*He rips it in half.*)

BILLINS: Hey Ronnie!

(RONNIE *rips it into quarters, then into little pieces.*)

BILLINS: I was meaning to hold onto that.

BROWFIELD: That wasn't your property, Ronnie.

RONNIE: I have a confession to make.

BROWFIELD: (*Uneasy*) What ... confession?

RONNIE: I've got to bare my soul, you know. It's about time, don't you think.

BROWFIELD: If you say so, Ronnie.

RONNIE: So family, dear family, there's something I must tell you all now.

BILLINS: What, Ronnie?

RONNIE: I'm on the verge of chucking veterinary medicine.

BILLINS: Oh, Ronnie.

ROSE: Talk him out of it, Bijou.

ACT ONE

BROWFIELD: But Ronnie, I thought you loved the ins and outs of animal anatomy.

RONNIE: I did, Browfield, once. Especially dogs. I loved them the best. Everything about them. You see, somehow, a dog is very pure, his essence. (*He seems to be on the verge of tears.*) No matter how humble he is, no matter ... his essence is always so pure, kind and unfathomable.

BROWFIELD: Sure, Ronnie.

RONNIE: But then I realized that I didn't have it in me, that pure essence, that ... whatever it is, mine was ... nothing left. (*He starts to sob.*) What's the use, huh? That's what I kept saying. What's the use of going near it anymore?

BROWFIELD: You know, Ronnie, you're doing a good job embarrassing us all.

RONNIE: You lousy fuck!

(*He leaps at* BROWFIELD. BILLINS *grabs him and holds him.*)

BILLINS: Ronnie! Ronnie!

RONNIE: (*Struggling*) Just a few seconds! I just wantta fuckin' kill him that's all!

BILLINS: It's Uncle Brow, it's only Uncle Brow.

RONNIE: Just wantta fuck him up bad!

BROWFIELD: Don't worry, Bijou, I can take care of myself.

ROSE: (*Going over to him*) Oh, Son, they've worked you too hard at the State University.

(RONNIE *stops struggling.* BILLINS *lets him go.*)

RONNIE: They have, Mom. They really have.

ROSE: Are they mean?

(*At this point we are not sure if* RONNIE *is playing a game with them or not.*)

RONNIE: Yes, they are. People don't realize. They drive you mercilessly there, Mom. (*Pause*) They have agents all over the place.

ROSE: What?

RONNIE: Scruntinizing your homework. Checking your reading habits.

ROSE: That's going too far.

RONNIE: Going through your old underwear.

ROSE: That's disgusting.

RONNIE: They have rooms there, Mom, that no living person has ever seen before.

ROSE: What, what goes on there?

RONNIE: Experiments that would be impossible to describe in human terms on this earth.

ROSE: Oh, Ronnie.

RONNIE: (*Very intense*) Screams—leave you screaming yourself, inside yourself, for hours and hours after you hear them. All in the name of science.

BILLINS: Does the State know about this, Ronnie?

RONNIE: Just between you and me, swearing to secrecy?

BILLINS: Sure, Ronnie.

RONNIE: I'm convinced that they do.

BILLINS: That's terrible. Isn't it, Brow?

BROWFIELD: It certainly is.

ROSE: Let's go inside now, Ronnie, and lie down and talk like we used to; and you can be a happy young man like you used to forever and ever.

RONNIE: That sounds great, Mom.

(*They start to walk off together. Suddenly* RONNIE *stops.*)

You are my Mommie, aren't you?

ROSE: I'm your God-given Mommie.

RONNIE: Then let's slap five!

ROSE: (*Perplexed*) What?

(RONNIE *turns over her hand and "slaps five".*)

RONNIE: Mommie.

ROSE: Son. (*To the others*) He's a spiffy one, isn't he?

BILLINS: He certainly is.

(*They go into the house together.*)

(JENNIFER *goes over to the swing and sits down.* LOU ANN *begins pacing around.* BILLINS *stretches and starts looking around for birds.* BROWFIELD *seems to be considering something.*)

LOU ANN: (*Stops pacing*) This is certainly an interesting family you've got here, Mr. Billins.

BILLINS: Never a dull moment.

BROWFIELD: Why don't you take a walk and enjoy the scenery, Lou Ann?

LOU ANN: There isn't any.

BROWFIELD: Well, I guess you can't have everything, now can you? (*He chuckles.*)

LOU ANN: I guess you can't. (*She walks around toward the front of the house and exits.*)

(BILLINS *begins rummaging intensely through his pockets.* BROWFIELD *watches him for a few moments.*)

BROWFIELD: What are you looking for?

BILLINS: (*Stares at him for a few moments.*) I don't know. I must have just forgot.

(BROWFIELD *shakes his head. Silence for a few moments.*)

BILLINS: We've had some great times, Bijou. But we've not yet come into our own.

BILLINS: We haven't?

BROWFIELD: Not by a long shot. So be prepared.

BILLINS: I certainly will.

BROWFIELD: The opportunities are limitless.

BILLINS: Name one.

BROWFIELD: Take Jennifer, for instance.

BILLINS: I don't go for her.

(BROWFIELD *goes over to* JENNIFER. *She is on the swing, swinging gently back and forth. She is completely lost in her own world.*)

BROWFIELD: Right. But there are others, Bijou, who find her more appealing, or scintillating.

BILLINS: I don't find her scintillating.

(BROWFIELD *helps her off the swing, then taking her by the hand leads her over to* BILLINS.)

BROWFIELD: Some of us though ... our feelings are like ... you like cutting through things sharp, like meat?

BILLINS: What?

BROWFIELD: (*Almost over the edge now, an animal. His hands start roaming all over her body.*) Some of us could do anything we want to her. Anything, anything—giving a great pleasure.

BILLINS: (*Impassive*) I guess so.

BROWFIELD: No liberty would be any liberty. Nothing would be enough. We'd keep cutting through the meat, you know, hunting up the desert.

BILLINS: I can see that.

BROWFIELD: I mean, strip her naked, Bijou. Strip her bare and stick her on top of the house like a weathervane.

BILLINS: That'd be funny.

BROWFIELD: And there she'd spin in all kinds of weather, the hail and rain and wind slapping against her, slapping her this way, slapping her that way, slapping her silly.

BILLINS: Why don't you do it, Brow?

BROWFIELD: I don't know if you'll be able to understand this, Bijou: but it is enough for me to know that I can do it, if the need arises.

BILLINS: I can understand that. (*Pause*) Still, I think you should try it, some really rainy afternoon or something.

BROWFIELD: Right now, Bijou, I am content ... just being ... (*He begins to caress her face.*) just being generous, loving, kind. I...

(Jennifer *bites his hand savagely.*)

Ahhhhh!

JENNIFER: (*Crying out*) Come down on them, Willie! Come down on them all! Flatten them, Willie!

BROWFIELD: Fuck!

JENNIFER: Flatten them! (*She races off.*) Willie! Willie!

BROWFIELD: She's a real bitch of a biter, that little whore.

BILLINS: It looks like she really nailed you, Brow.

BROWFIELD: Ahh, shut up. (*He takes out a handkerchief and begins to wrap it around his hand.*)

(*Silence for a few moments.* ROSE *appears at the window.*)

ROSE: Yoo hoo, boys.

BILLINS: How's Ronnie, Rose?

ROSE: He's sleeping like a little puppy.

BILLINS: That's nice, Rose.

ROSE: Guess what I just found in the fridge, Brow?

BROWFIELD: Homemade brownies.

ROSE: Ohhh, you're such a smart aleck. But try and guess what else I found there.

BROWFIELD: Rose, I'm absolutely stymied.

ROSE: Fudge sauce!

BROWFIELD: Not fudge sauce?

ROSE: Fudge sauce! So why don't you come inside and help me yummy yum them up.

BROWFIELD: I'd love to yummy up your brownies, Rose.

(*She giggles.*)

But don't let's tell Bijou about it. (*He starts to tip-toe out.*)

ROSE: Not a word.

(*At this point* BILLINS *seems oblivious. He mutters to himself and starts to search through his pockets, but stops when he is unable to remember what he is looking for. Now he looks up into the sky.*)

BILLINS: Hey, look at that big robin up there. With that funny snake thing in his mouth.

(*The lights start to dim and then go out.*)

END OF ACT ONE

ACT TWO

(*That evening. The interior of an animal hospital.*)

(*The lights come up.* RONNIE *is operating on a dog. We now hear something, a presence: some rustling, movement, maybe some scratching, breathing.* RONNIE *stops working and listens. The sounds disappear. Now he goes back to work; once more he hears the sounds. He stops. He is about to go to the door and check, but then decides not to. The sounds disappear. He goes back to work. After a few moments the sounds return, this time louder, more insistent, overpowering. He thinks he may be going crazy. The scalpel slips from his hand. Suddenly the front door opens and* LOU ANN *enters. The sounds stop.*)

LOU ANN: Hi, Ronnie.

(*He just stares at her.*)

Oh, Ronnie. I thought you were feeling better.

RONNIE: I was, Lou Ann.

LOU ANN: Then what happened?

RONNIE: I had a setback.

LOU ANN: What caused it?

RONNIE: I'd rather not talk about it.

LOU ANN: You know, Ronnie, maybe I should go back home.

RONNIE: No, Lou Ann.

LOU ANN: It's not that we've known each other that long.

RONNIE: Over a month.

LOU ANN: I mean, we're not going steady or anything.

RONNIE: But we're going, aren't we? We're still going.

LOU ANN: Yes, we're going.

RONNIE: (*Loooking around*) You know, sometimes I give myself the chills. (*Pause*) I know I kind of act weird sometimes.

LOU ANN: Well...

RONNIE: Hard to put up with.

LOU ANN: I'm hanging in there, though.

RONNIE: (*Suddenly, with a sweeping gesture*) How do you like my domain?

LOU ANN: (*Looking around*) It's creepy.

RONNIE: It belongs to Dr. Mulvaney. Not the most modern facility in the state, I'll grant you.

LOU ANN: It smells funny.

RONNIE: Not the cleanest facility in the state. Dr. Mulvaney is a bit of a juice head, you see.

LOU ANN: He sounds delightful.

RONNIE: Oh, he's got some good points, believe me. He took me in.

LOU ANN: What do you mean?

RONNIE: A long time ago, when Willie ... after Willie ... left.

LOU ANN: Oh.

RONNIE: I started hanging around here, helping out. It reminded me of Willie somehow, some part of Willie, anyway. I felt peaceful.

LOU ANN: I was just talking to your mother about Willie.

RONNIE: (*On the edge*) Shut up about my mother.

LOU ANN: Hey, Ronnie, I'm just...

RONNIE: (*Trying to take it back*) I mean we all know she's a bit daffy.

LOU ANN: She's certainly not the only one I've noticed.

ACT TWO

RONNIE: Of course. I mean, this is an authentic American family.

LOU ANN: What do you mean?

RONNIE: It's real, no shit, seething, no holds barred, you know what I mean?

LOU ANN: I guess.

RONNIE: It's a crap shoot. The stakes are high. It's ... No. The game's over. We know who the winners are. We know who the losers are.

LOU ANN: It can't be as pat as that, can it?

RONNIE: I used to know a girl named Pat. She had flaming red hair. She died in a motorcycle accident.

LOU ANN: Ronnie.

RONNIE: Ahh, come on. Don't take me too seriously.

LOU ANN: But I do take you seriously.

RONNIE: The only things I take seriously are things eternal.

LOU ANN: Like what?

RONNIE: Like this. (*He howls*)

LOU ANN: Geez.

RONNIE: You like the way I do that?

LOU ANN: I don't know.

RONNIE: Wantta hear it again?

LOU ANN: I'm not certain.

(*He howls again.*)

Jezzzusssss.

RONNIE: I love when they do that. It pricks up the hair on the back of my neck. (*He grabs her and pulls her to him.*) It pricks me right up. Know what I mean?

LOU ANN: Yeah.

RONNIE: Ever do it in an animal hospital?

LOU ANN: It smells of piss in here.

RONNIE: Oh, hoity toity.

LOU ANN: I didn't say it turned me off.

RONNIE: (*Staring at her*) We may have some kind of ... destiny ... going for us, you know.

LOU ANN: Yeah, maybe.

RONNIE: So maybe we should just ... stay with it, you know ... right to the final outcome.

LOU ANN: Piss is not the worst smell in the world.

RONNIE: (*Looks at her and smiles.*) I've got an operation to contend with. (*He turns away from her.*)

LOU ANN: Ronnie.

RONNIE: What's up?

LOU ANN: Do you mind if I ask you a question ... about Willie?

RONNIE: (*Hesitating for a moment.*) Ask your heart out.

LOU ANN: Is Willie a dead person, Ronnie?

(*He stares at her. She holds her ground.*)

Is he a dead person, Ronnie?

RONNIE: Yeah, he is. As dead as the dead can get.

LOU ANN: All right.

RONNIE: Fucking totally. (*Starts to laugh*) I mean, what did you expect? How could a live person have the kind of power that Willie has, you dumb bitch?

LOU ANN: Watch it, Ronnie.

RONNIE: I mean, the average live person coming down the pike is a flaming asshole.

LOU ANN: Some of them.

RONNIE: Most of them, in my book. But Willie ... he was something else; he was connected to the prime. He wasn't like any other living person that you've ever seen; he was on fire with the prime. You'd know it in a fucking second. You'd feel things touch you inside out, like you never had before. Do you understand?

LOU ANN: Yeah.

RONNIE: Do you follow me?

LOU ANN: Let's go somewhere else, Ronnie, away from this blood-piss place.

RONNIE: (*Staring hard at her*) I've got a dog here.

LOU ANN: What?

RONNIE: (*Pointing to the dog*) This dog here, this dog lying in limbo waiting for me. I mean, he might not look like much, but some kid loves him as much as you loved your little brother.

LOU ANN: Then fix him up.

RONNIE: Just don't tell me what to do, all right?

LOU ANN: Jeeezzzzusssss.

RONNIE: (*Pause*) What did my mother tell you about Willie?

LOU ANN: She said, they found him, a farmer found him up in the hills with his sheep.

(RONNIE *laughs*.)

Was she hallucinating, Ronnie?

RONNIE: No. She was talking God's truth.

LOU ANN: She said the farmer was a friend of the family, and wasn't married, so he gave him to your family to take care of for a while.

RONNIE: Willie was about four or five at the time. He couldn't speak.

LOU ANN: She didn't tell me that.

RONNIE: Not for about a year, anyway; and then when he did it was kind of incredible, unbelievable. After a while he got to sound like the rest of us, but at the beginning...

LOU ANN: And that he was protected by this really fierce dog.

RONNIE: Yeah. When they found him there was this incredible dog watching over him. (*Pause*) He didn't last two weeks.

LOU ANN: What happened to him?

RONNIE: My father ran him over with the pickup truck.

LOU ANN: Shit.

RONNIE: He was left without protection. He was trapped in this family. You see, we're all trapped by these families. It's like a net. But...

(*Silence*)

LOU ANN: What, Ronnie?

RONNIE: He was no fucking angel, believe me.

LOU ANN: What do you mean.

RONNIE: (*Almost to himself*) But when we were small I thought he was ... some kind ... of angel ... some something else ... or something ... (*Pause*) When we were teenagers all kind of hell broke loose. I mean, we were like other teenagers but more so. I was completely under his spell in those days.

LOU ANN: What kind of stuff went on?

RONNIE: All kinds of shit—like we took on Browfield was one of the things.

LOU ANN: What happened?

RONNIE: We squeezed his tit for thousands of dollars.

LOU ANN: What do you mean?

RONNIE: Blackmailed him.

ACT TWO

LOU ANN: Christ!

RONNIE: I mean, I didn't do that much. It was mainly Willie and Jennifer.

LOU ANN: Jennifer?

RONNIE: Yeah, in those days she had a lot more ... on the ball.

LOU ANN: I didn't know.

RONNIE: I got some money out of it, though. I bought a motorcycle with my loot.

LOU ANN: What did Willie and Jennifer do?

RONNIE: They took off to New Orleans for a couple of weeks. They had the time of their lives.

(LOU ANN *laughs.*)

We brought off unbelievable things. (*He goes over to the dog and begins to stroke him.*) Look at this beast. He's in limbo. He waits for me to save him. (*Pause*) Willie was this small creature who was found in the hills among animals; and my family took him in, and decided to protect him, and made him a foster child. (*Pause*) It was a big mistake.

LOU ANN: Oh, Ronnie.

RONNIE: I'm going to kill this dog. (*Pause*) They were out to get Willie. Somewhere along the line they just decided it. Before he had ever done anything to them. One day I overheard them plotting. There was no reason for it. They ... (*Suddenly angry*) But maybe they knew something I didn't know?

LOU ANN: What?

RONNIE: I mean, I was just a kid. Maybe they saw his blacked out planets before I did? Maybe they were really on to something after all?

LOU ANN: I doubt it.

RONNIE: What the hell do you know!

LOU ANN: From what I've heard...

RONNIE: He had no mercy. He could do terrible things.

LOU ANN: Listen, Ronnie, I just think...

RONNIE: I don't want any more goddamn fucking sympathy for him! It's disgusting. Like once—I'll tell you the truth—he had these dogs bite me.

LOU ANN: What dogs?

RONNIE: All dogs. Any dogs that were around. He was pissed off at me, so he'd just get these hounds to bite me.

(*She stares at him.*)

Bite the shit out of me! No kidding, Lou Ann. It took me years to get back into the good graces of dogs.

LOU ANN: That's the craziest thing I've ever heard.

RONNIE: (*Smiling*) So why the fuck don't you go back to College Town?

LOU ANN: What do you mean?

RONNIE: Where things are more to your liking. (*He turns to the dog and picks up his scalpel.*) You know, there's some little freckle-faced kid at home now saying: "How's Bowzer? Is Bowzer gonna make it, Dad? When's Bowzer gonna come home again and play?" Well, I'll tell you, Lou Ann, it's too much, it's just too goddamn fucking much for me to bear. (*He begins stabbing the dog with the scalpel.*)

LOU ANN: Ronnie!

(*He finishes and stands there, staring at the dog.*)

RONNIE: Hate to tell you this son, but Bowzer went down under the knife.

(JENNIFER *steps out from behind the cages. She is holding a notebook and a pencil in her hand.*)

(*Terrified*) Oh, shit! What the hell are you doing here? (*Rushing to her*) Beat it, Jennifer. (*He grabs her.*) Get the hell out.

ACT TWO

JENNIFER: (*Struggling*) Nooooo. (*She scratches him across the neck.*)

(RONNIE *cries out and hits her hard, knocking her down.*)

LOU ANN: You bastard! (*Going to* JENNIFER) Let me help you up. (*She gives her a hand, helping her up.*)

JENNIFER: My pencil point is broken.

LOU ANN: You're a creep, Ronnie.

RONNIE: Yeah, well, Jennifer can take it. She's part of the family.

LOU ANN: Great family.

RONNIE: You find it disagreeable, do you?

LOU ANN: That's right.

RONNIE: Then why don't you beat it?

LOU ANN: Good idea. (*She starts looking for her coat.*) You know, Ronnie, I never want to see you again.

RONNIE: That goes double for me.

(*She starts to exit.*)

That goes just about fucking double for me, Lou Ann. (*Crying out*) You know that, Lou Ann? Double!

(*She is gone now,*)

JENNIFER: Poor Ronnie.

RONNIE: I'm no good inside, Jennifer.

(*The sound of thunder is heard.*)

JENNIFER: You're just hurt, Ronnie.

(*Enormous thunder sounds are heard, and lightning flashes seen outside the windows; rain comes crashing down.*)

RONNIE: No, I just ... take ... (*He grabs her wrist.*) take what I need to get by. (*He throws her down, getting on top of her.*)

JENNIFER: You can't hurt me, Ronnie.

RONNIE: Bet?

JENNIFER: Yes, I'll bet you.

RONNIE: Then tell me why I can't hurt you.

JENNIFER: Because I love you so.

RONNIE: Don't say that, Jennifer.

JENNIFER: (*Caressing his face*) Because all things say I love you so.

RONNIE: Jennifer...

JENNIFER: All things say I love you so, all things. (*She keeps repeating these words, at the same time holding him, caressing him, rocking him.*)

RONNIE: No, Jennifer. Please, Jennifer. No, Jennifer.

(*Silence now. Then thunder. Silence.*)

(*Now* RONNIE *sits up.*)

RONNIE: I'm going under, Jennifer.

JENNIFER: Oh, Ronnie. (*She gets up.*)

RONNIE: I can't hang on much longer. I can't. (*He gets up and walks over to the dog and touches it.*)

(*Now the door opens and* BILLINS *enters. He is wearing an old rubber raincoat and hat, and is dripping wet. He immediately sees* JENNIFER.)

BILLINS: What's she doing here?

RONNIE: Ahh, shove it.

BILLINS: What'd you say, Ronnie?

RONNIE: I said: She just dropped over for a chat.

BILLINS: But she knows that this place is off limits to her.

RONNIE: Maybe she forgot.

BILLINS: Did you forget that this place was off limits to you, Jennifer?

ACT TWO

JENNIFER: No. I remembered exactly, but I decided to come anyway.

(BILLINS *shakes his head and mutters.*)

(*The rain begins to subside.*)

JENNIFER: (*To* RONNIE) I'm going outside and look around for Willie.

BILLINS: Give him my best if you run into him.

JENNIFER: (*Laughing*) He really hates you. (*She starts to exit.*) Bye, Ronnie.

RONNIE: Bye.

(*She is gone.*)

(BILLINS *is looking at the dog.*)

BILLINS: What's the matter with this dog, Ronnie?

RONNIE: Nothing.

BILLINS: He looks like he's dead.

RONNIE: He's not. He's just playing dead.

BILLINS: Oh.

RONNIE: He's a very smart dog.

BILLINS: Mmmmmmm. (*Pause*) You gotta come home with me now, Ronnie.

RONNIE: Why?

BILLINS: Your mother needs you in a urgent way. She's been calling for you.

RONNIE: Why?

BILLINS: She's been seeing you-know-who again. She needs your support. You've got to be advised that this is not one of her greatest days.

RONNIE: I'm advised.

BILLINS: Well, are you coming home?

RONNIE: I've got to clean up around here first, don't I?

BILLINS: I guess you do. (*He starts to leave.*) I'll be waiting on pins and needles for you, Ronnie.

RONNIE: Yeah.

(BILLINS *exits.*)

(RONNIE *goes over to the refrigerator and takes out a can of beer. Now he closes the refrigerator and goes over to the operating table, sitting down on a stool. He opens the beer, begins to drink, and starts talking to the dog.*)

RONNIE: You're better off, aren't you, aren't you? (*He growls playfully.*) Lots better off. No more begging and doing stupid tricks, no more getting whacked with newspapers. Dog heaven ... just one big field to pee and romp rabbits in. I mean, I've done you a favor.

(*Suddenly we are aware of a presence: breathing, movement, maybe some scratching.*)

What is it? (*He looks around, frightened.*) Come on. Get out of here.

(*The sound grows in intensity.*)

Come on! Stop the shit! (*Suddenly smiles*) All right, all right. (*Swigs some beer*) You're not going to bother me. It's not going to bother me. (*He turns on the radio. Rock music begins to play loudly.*) We're going to have a party! All right, all you demon denizens of the animal world, come on, come on! (*He begins banging cages. The dogs start barking.*) Let's all rock 'n roll. (*He begins dancing around.*) Let's all...

(*The lights begin to flicker on and off.*)

What? Geezzzzzussss. ...

(*Blackness*)

Christ! What's going on?

(*We hear a voice in the darkness.*)

VOICE: Storm must have hit the power.

RONNIE: Oh, no.

ACT TWO

(A crash. Long silence, then the lights come back up. The music is off. The dogs are silent. WILLIE *stands on one side of the room facing* RONNIE. *He wears old clothes as if he had been on the road a long time. A pack is slung over his back. His left eye is gone. His right arm is gone. There are scars on his face. He gives the impression of a fragile, broken, but still powerful animal.)*

(The two men stand there a long time, staring at each other.)

WILLIE: You've changed, Ronnie.

RONNIE: No, I haven't, Willie. I never change.

WILLIE: That's not true, Ronnie.

RONNIE: But you, Willie, you...

WILLIE: I've been altered. *(Smiles slightly)*

RONNIE: Yeah. You have, you have.

WILLIE: Can you stand looking at it, Ronnie?

RONNIE: I dont' know.

WILLIE: See if you can. See what you can do. *(He begins walking toward him.)*

RONNIE: No more, Willie

(WILLIE *keeps coming.*)

(RONNIE *cries out.*) Willie, I said no more!

(Blackout. A blinding flash of light. Darkness. The lights come back up. The men are in different positions in the room, standing about five feet away from each other.)

WILLIE: I don't know what happened. There was no plan or anything. I was just ... circling through the country ... and all of a sudden I found myself less than a hundred miles from this place.

RONNIE: Oh, Willie.

WILLIE: I couldn't pass it up, now could I?

RONNIE: You could have.

WILLIE: I couldn't pass up my family, now could I, Ronnie?

RONNIE: Oh, fuck it, Willie.

WILLIE: You see my wounds have never healed. Never properly. And I suffer more, with my wounds and all, not properly healed.

RONNIE: So you thought coming back here would help matters?

WILLIE: Back to this family that...

RONNIE: It wasn't a family!

WILLIE: What?

RONNIE: It wasn't a true family to you!

WILLIE: What about you, Ronnie, was it a true family to you?

RONNIE: Yes, it was, it was.

(WILLIE *laughs*.)

For Christ's sake it was, Willie!

(*Blackout. A blinding flash of light. Darkness. The lights come back up and the men are in different positions in the room.*)

(RONNIE *goes to the refrigerator and takes out two beers. He opens them and offers one to* WILLIE. WILLIE *takes it. Both men drink long and slowly. Now they lower their beers and cry out—a wild animal cry—and embrace.*)

RONNIE: I don't want to say I missed you, Willie. I don't want to.

(*Blackout. A blinding flash of light. Darkness. The lights come back up and the men are in different positions in the room.*)

WILLIE: Where's Jennifer?

RONNIE: You know...

WILLIE: What?

ACT TWO 57

RONNIE: She's around. She's been around all these years.

WILLIE: I figured that.

RONNIE: But, Willie ... she's not like ... she was.

WILLIE: Yeah.

RONNIE: What do you mean?

WILLIE: I just know that, Ronnie. I just knew.

RONNIE: Take off now, Willie. I'll give you some money. Come on. We'll find Jennifer, then you'll go.

WILLIE: I just blew into town, Ronnie.

RONNIE: Blow out of it, Willie. It's dangerous here. Believe me.

WILLIE: I don't care.

RONNIE: I know you don't. But I do.

WILLIE: Not yet. It's not my time.

RONNIE: Willie!

WILLIE: What?

RONNIE: I'm glad you're alive.

WILLIE: Are you?

RONNIE: I don't know. Maybe I'm just guessing. Maybe after you're gone the thought of it will finish me ... so ... please, Willie ... hit the fucking road to the ends of any place but here.

(*The door opens and* ROSE *enters. At first she thinks that* RONNIE'S *alone.*)

ROSE: Oh, Ronnie, I'm glad you're here. I just couldn't stay cooped up with that man anymore. I ... (*Noticing* WILLIE) Oh, you have a friend here. Is he another veterinarian scholar, Ronnie?

RONNIE: Rose, I'd like you to meet a very dear old friend...

(WILLIE *steps into the light.*)

ROSE: WILLIE! (*She slumps back onto a chair, or the edge of the operating table.*)

ROSE: Aaaaaaaa.

WILLIE: I'm going to get Jennifer now. It'll be all right, Ronnie. Don't worry.

RONNIE: Yeah, sure.

(WILLIE *exits.*)

ROSE: I can't believe it.

(RONNIE *goes and gets another beer, opens it, and starts to drink.*)

RONNIE: I've got work to do, Rose.

ROSE: Tell me—I may be amazed or losing my sight—but was there something incredibly wrong with his body?

RONNIE: Yeah, there was something incredibly wrong with his body.

ROSE: What was it, Ronnie?

RONNIE: His arm is gone, and his eye is out.

ROSE: Despicable! That's the most vile, despicable thing I ever heard. Leave it to Willie to continually sicken us.

RONNIE: (*Softly, calmly*) I could strangle you right now. You know, do it slowly, but do it thoroughly.

(*She stares at him, not sure what he is saying.*)

RONNIE: Hear you gasp your last—it would be so pleasurable.

(*The door opens and* BILLINS *enters.*)

BILLINS: Oh, Rose, I'm glad you're here.

(*She turns away from him.*)

BILLINS: I looked high and low. (*Pause*) Funny thing, as I was driving up I saw someone walking out, looking familiar.

ROSE: You cancelled postage stamp.

ACT TWO 59

BILLINS: What?

ROSE: You cancelled little object.

(BILLINS *looks at* RONNIE *and shrugs.*)

Willie!

BILLINS: What?

RONNIE: She says that was Willie walking out.

BILLINS: Ahhh, Ronnie, between you and me and the lamppost, she's been saying...

RONNIE: Listen to this because I'm only going to tell you once: Willie just walked out of here, with a pack of Chesterfields in his shirt pocket, alert and alive.

ROSE: Willie!

BILLINS: If you say so, Ronnie.

RONNIE: I say so. (*He takes out a cigarette and offers one to the dog.*) Like a smoke? (*Listening to the dog*) Oh, I see. You quit.

ROSE: Stop that, Ronnie.

RONNIE: (*To the dog*) I wish I could quit. (*He lights up a cigarette.*)

BILLINS: So you and your mother both...

RONNIE: Look, if you don't want to believe me, don't believe me.

BILLINS: I didn't say I didn't believe you; just...

RONNIE: I'll give you a contact high. (*He begins blowing smoke in the dog's face.*)

ROSE: (*To* BILLINS) Well, do something!

BILLINS: What am I supposed to do, Rose?

ROSE: Call Browfield.

BILLINS: What should I tell him?

ROSE: Tell him the truth.

BILLINS: That's just what I'll do, Rose. (*He goes into the other room to make the phone call.*)

(ROSE *begins praying to Jesus, mumbling softly, somewhat incoherently, to herself.*)

RONNIE: (*Laughs*) He told me a joke.

ROSE: Now, stop that, Ronnie.

(BILLINS *sticks his head in from the other room.*)

BILLINS: He doesn't believe me, Rose.

ROSE: Tell him he better believe you.

BILLINS: All right, Rose. (*He withdraws his head.*)

(RONNIE *begins barking loudly.*)

ROSE: Stop that, Ronnie. (*She resumes praying.*)

(*The door opens and* LOU ANN *enters. She is covered with mud from head to foot.*)

LOU ANN: Hey, Ronnie, what's happening?

RONNIE: Hey, Lou Ann, look's like you got some mud on your make-up.

LOU ANN: You see, Ronnie, I slipped and fell in the mud out there; but instead of getting right up, I didn't. And I also kind of rolled around a bit.

(ROSE *makes a sound of exasperation.*)

RONNIE: Did you like it?

LOU ANN: I did like it. I liked it a lot. (*Pause*) There's something out there.

RONNIE: I know there is, babe.

(BILLINS *enters.*)

BILLINS: Well, I convinced him. He'll be right over. You oughta go home and wash up, Lou Ann. You'd be better off.

LOU ANN: I want to meet him, Ronnie.

ACT TWO   61

RONNIE: Do you?

LOU ANN: I know he's here somewhere.

RONNIE: You'll meet him, but first ... (*He takes her by the hand and begins leading her somewhere.*)

BILLINS: Where are you going, Ronnie?

RONNIE: I'm taking Lou Ann behind the cages, so we can have sex together.

BILLINS: Ronnie, your mother is right here. Standing here.

ROSE: (*To* BILLINS) Did you put the meatloaf away like I asked you, or is it still on the stove?

BILLINS: I think still on the stove, Rose.

ROSE: (*Shaking her head*) I can't believe it. I cannot believe it.

BILLINS: It won't spoil.

(*The door opens, and* WILLIE *and* JENNIFER *enter.*)

LOU ANN: Oh, Jeez.

RONNIE: He's found her.

JENNIFER: (*Beaming*) Look everybody, look who I ran into outside.

ROSE: Lucky you.

JENNIFER: It's Willie, our dear Willie. A little different but the same as ever.

RONNIE: Willie, I want you to meet Lou Ann.

LOU ANN: Hello, Willie.

WILLIE: You're Ronnie's friend, are you?

LOU ANN: Yes, Willie. I am.

WILLIE: That's good.

BILLINS: Boy, oh boy, oh boy. It's Willie. (*He goes over to* WILLIE *and is about to shake his hand, then noticing his condition seems confused and steps back.*) How are you, Willie?

WILLIE: More so than ever, Bijou.

BILLINS: That's nice. Did you hear that, Rose?

ROSE: Just passing through, are you, Willie?

(*He just stares at her.*)

BILLINS: Travel has always been a pleasure that I haven't been able to bother with.

ROSE: But with Willie I'll bet travel has long been a part of his comings and goings.

WILLIE: Why don't you shut up, Rose?

BILLINS: Now, Willie, you'll just have to...

WILLIE: You, too, Bijou.

(BILLINS *stops dead.*)

ROSE: One question, Willie, just one tiny baby question.

WILLIE: What is it, Rose?

ROSE: Why aren't you dead, Willie?

BILLINS: Rose!

ROSE: I have a right to ask, Bijou.

WILLIE: She has her rights, Billins.

ROSE: See, Willie agrees. (*Sweetly*) So why aren't you completely dead, Willie?

WILLIE: Gee, Rose.

ROSE: It's a serious thing to escape from an authentic and certifiable death. Maybe even a terrible crime.

WILLIE: Could be.

ROSE: And you're missing out on so much, Willie.

WILLIE: How do you see that, Rose?

ROSE: Well, Willie, right now I'm sure you'd be in a very nice place, a place much nicer than this in all its

ACT TWO

wonder. It'd be all pink and soft. And you could sleep as late as you want in the morning. And angels would come walking around all day playing the most popular songs on their guitars and mandolins.

WILLIE: You paint a beautiful picture, Rose.

BILLINS: *(Smiling)* She certainly does, doesn't she?

ROSE: So, Willie, why...

WILLIE: Because I didn't want to be dead, Rose.

BILLINS: Do you mind if I drink one of these beers here, Ronnie?

RONNIE: Go right ahead.

(BILLINS *opens a can and begins to drink.*)

BILLINS: Mmmmmm, mmmmm. Nice cold beer.

ROSE: I hate him when he drinks.

BILLINS: Mmmmmm.

(BROWFIELD *enters.*)

ROSE: (*To* BILLINS) Thank God he's here.

BROWFIELD: *(Staring at* WILLIE) Willie, Willie, Willie, do these old eyes deceive me?

WILLIE: No, they don't.

BROWFIELD: It's so good seeing you again.

WILLIE: It's sweet here too, Browfield.

(BROWFIELD *enters the room.*)

BROWFIELD: I've never been one to mince words or beat around the bush, Willie; ... so ... (*He takes out an envelope from his jacket.*) We've taken up a collection.

BILLINS: Who did?

ROSE: Quiet down.

BROWFIELD: For a new start, Willie.

WILLIE: I've already had my start, Browfield.

BROWFIELD: You can never have too many of those, Willie.

WILLIE: One's all I ever wanted, Browfield.

BROWFIELD: Willie, Willie come on. It's been all so many years ago. Everything's changed since then. Look at me, for instance: so much more warm, soft, human than I'd ever been before.

ROSE: Like cheese.

BILLINS: Like a cheese sandwich.

BROWFIELD: (*Laughing*) See, Willie, they know. They know the truth. And now it's your turn: Know the truth, Willie, know it for what it is.

JENNIFER: Willie and I are going to New Orleans and listen to music.

LOU ANN: (*Takes the money from* BROWFIELD.) Take the money, Willie. Please. Take it and get out of here. (*She stares at him.*) I love you and Ronnie both, Willie.

WILLIE: Ronnie's coming with us to New Orleans.

RONNIE: Not on your life.

WILLIE: I think you'll change your mind, Ronnie.

LOU ANN: Go with him, Ronnie. We'll all go.

RONNIE: I've got too many dead dogs to work on here, Willie. They need me.

BROWFIELD: What you've got going for you in that envelope, Willie, is five big ones. And if you take it right now, what you're going to have riding along with it is a matching fund of another five thou', which I have at this moment sequestered in my car.

WILLIE: Take it, Jennifer.

(JENNIFER *takes the money from* LOU ANN.)

Count it, Jennifer.

ACT TWO

(*She counts the money.*)

Now tear it up, Jennifer.

BROWFIELD: What?

(*She begins to tear up the money.*)

(BROWFIELD *makes a move to stop her, then thinks better of it.*)

BROWFIELD: Okay, Willie. Okay fucking Willie.

WILLIE: Tear it up real good, Jennifer.

JENNIFER: Real nice and tiny.

WILLIE: Now give them a party, Jennifer. Make them happy.

JENNIFER: Happy Birthday, boys and girls! (*She throws the money into the air.*)

(BILLINS *goes down on his hands and knees and starts to pick up the pieces.*)

BROWFIELD: What the hell are you doing?

BILLINS: I hate to see it just lying there like that, Brow.

BROWFIELD: Get up, will you.

ROSE: (*Whispering*) You'll take care of it later.

(*The lights change on* WILLIE. *He assumes an animal form, and begins to glide about the room, hunting for something. The dogs growl softly. Everybody moves out of his way. After a while he comes back to his human form.*)

WILLIE: (*Grabbing hold of* RONNIE) Come on, Ronnie!

(ROSE *grabs* RONNIE.)

WILLIE: Get away from him, Rose.

ROSE: Willie, please...

WILLIE: You forget who I am, Rose?

ROSE: No. (*She lets go of him.*)

RONNIE: Leave me alone, Willie. (*He pulls away from him.*)

WILLIE: You forget who I am, Ronnie?

RONNIE: (*Crying out*) Yes!

WILLIE: No! You haven't!

LOU ANN: Ronnie knows who you are, Willie. He's never forgotten you or anything you've shown him.

RONNIE: Shut up, Lou Ann! (*To* WILLIE) I've forgotten everything, Willie, everything.

WILLIE: I don't believe that.

RONNIE: I just want to finish off here, Willie, where I began.

WILLIE: No. (*He turns to the others.*) Have you forgotten that I gave you Jesus, Rose?

ROSE: No. But it wasn't, wasn't really...

WILLIE: It was really Jesus. Jesus like you've never seen before, in the flesh, blood, and thorns.

ROSE: He was ... so close. He loved me so. He...

BILLINS: Stop it, Rose.

ROSE: Don't tell me anything! Ever! Ever!

BILLINS: I just think you oughta fence off the Jesus area a little bit, Rose.

ROSE: How about fencing you off a little bit instead?

BILLINS: That's not what I'm talking about, Rose.

ROSE: But before we do ... one sensible subject ... regarding those little children.

BILLINS: That's been a long time ago, Rose.

ROSE: Which ones did you like best: the little boys, or the little girls?

BILLINS: That's long past, Rose.

ROSE: How do I know you don't do it anymore?

ACT TWO

BILLINS: Word of honor.

ROSE: I wouldn't have known then, if Willie didn't show me.

WILLIE: I showed you the truth, Rose.

ROSE: You naked, watching them naked.

BILLINS: I never touched them, Auntie Rose.

ROSE: Disgusting.

BILLINS: Never once, never. (*Pause*) Just once or twice.

WILLIE: Tell her who you liked the best, Bijou.

BILLINS: Well, it's hard to say.

WILLIE: Tell her!

BILLINS: I liked them both, the little boys and the little girls—but mainly the boys.

ROSE: I knew it.

BILLINS: They're the ones I like the best.

ROSE: Disgusting.

BROWFIELD: What are you after, then, Willie?

WILLIE: Look what you did to him, and to me.

BROWFIELD: The past is forgotten, in my mind.

WILLIE: And to her. (*He points at* JENNIFER.)

BROWFIELD: Don't try to pin her on us, Willie. She was always over the line, riding into traffic.

BILLINS: And another thing, Rose.

ROSE: What are you saying to me?

BILLINS: You had Browfield.

ROSE: No!

BROWFIELD: Lay off, Bijou.

BILLINS: You and Rose had each other, Browfield.

ROSE: Not in any normal way!

BILLINS: Had, Rose, had.

ROSE: Because Jesus came and told me to go to Browfield —I had no choice.

BILLINS: Had, Rose, had.

ROSE: Not in any normal way!

BILLINS: Had!

BROWFIELD: Shut up, you fucking jerk!

BILLINS: I just want it made plain and clear, Brow. Had!

BROWFIELD: Just shut up, just ... (*He looks at* WILLIE.) He wants us to tear each other up. Don't you see that? (*He starts to laugh.*) Sure, sure. He's pulling all his old tricks again. He's ... (*Pause*) Speaking about "had" and "had-ing"...

WILLIE: What is it, Browfield?

BROWFIELD: I also "had" Jennifer.

WILLIE: Yes.

BROWFIELD: I "had" her any way I wanted her, as often as I wanted her.

JENNIFER: Oh, Willie.

WILLIE: Because I gave her to you.

BROWFIELD: Yes! Yes!

LOU ANN: Why'd you do it, Willie?

BROWFIELD: What a filthy pig! Don't you all agree?

BILLINS: I for sure agree.

WILLIE: Because I wanted to get the goods on them. Because I would have done anything to destroy them.

BROWFIELD: (*Furious*) Blackmailed the goddamn hell out of me! Still, still ... (*Calming down*) I had the woman he loved. I mean ... (*Smiling at* BILLINS) You know.

ACT TWO

BILLINS: I know.

BROWFIELD: Still, what can you think of a man like that, give the love of his heart away?

WILLIE: Not too damn much.

BROWFIELD: I'm glad you agree, my friend.

WILLIE: I went too far; but I would do it again, to drown you in your poison.

JENNIFER: It's okay, Willie. We got the goods on him.

BROWFIELD: Throw him out!

BILLINS: You're right.

BROWFIELD: I wouldn't give him the time of the day. Look at him, a bum, a pimp, a charlatan, a rip-off artist. Throw him out! The sacred Willie, the marvelous Willie—Ha! Throw him the fuck out on the interstate with the rest of the dead animals!

BILLINS: It'd be too good for him

WILLIE: Look over there in that dog cage, look who's coming to greet you.

BROWFIELD: Don't look, Rose!

WILLIE: It's Jesus, isn't it?

ROSE: Yes! It is!

BILLINS: Close your eyes, Rose!

WILLIE: I give you Jesus!

BROWFIELD: Save yourself, Rose!

WILLIE: I give you the living God!

ROSE: Aaaaaaaaa. (*Swooning, she falls backwards.* BILLINS *grabs her. She is still conscious though, staring at the apparition in front of her.*)

WILLIE: What about you, Bijou?

BILLINS: Leave me alone, Willie. (*He starts to beat it out of there.*)

WILLIE: Billins!

(BILLINS *stops dead, then turns toward* WILLIE.)

I gave you the perfect one, didn't I?

BILLINS: Please, Willie.

WILLIE: I brought you the perfect child to look upon.

BILLINS: Willie, no, Willie...

WILLIE: There, Bijou, there. He wants to see you, Bijou. Look. He's smiling at you, Bijou. Can you believe it?

BILLINS: I can. (*He falls under the spell of the apparition.*)

(WILLIE *turns toward* BROWFIELD.)

BROWFIELD: Keep the fuck away from me, Willie.

(WILLIE *begins walking toward him.*)

I'm warning you. I'm no weak-kneed, pussy moron, Willie! (*Crying out frantically*) I'm not. I'm not!

WILLIE: (*Advancing slowly toward him*) I gave you...

BROWFIELD: I'm no pussy!

WILLIE: I gave you Jennifer and I gave you Rose. But a Jennifer and a Rose that you had never seen before. Remember, Brow?

BROWFIELD: They were beautiful.

WILLIE: Your dreams had slipped out of your mind and become flesh.

BROWFIELD: Yes.

WILLIE: There, Brow. They've never forgotten you.

(BROWFIELD *cries out sharply and is trapped by the apparition.*)

(WILLIE *turns toward* RONNIE.)

RONNIE: You can't control me anymore, Willie.

ACT TWO 71

WILLIE: I still have power over you, Ronnie.

RONNIE: Maybe you do. But I'm going to ask you to do it my way.

WILLIE: What way is that?

RONNIE: "One arm."

LOU ANN: What are you going to do, Ronnie?

WILLIE: All right, all right.

(RONNIE *walks into the middle of the room.* WILLIE *follows him. Now* RONNIE *turns towards him, his right arm behind his back, his left arm extended.*)

LOU ANN: Don't do it, Ronnie.

(WILLIE *extends his left arm. Now they circle around one another, dueling. They feint, attack, withdraw.*)

JENNIFER: Don't worry, Lou Ann, the boys are just playing.

(*Gradually the attacks grow more intense, rapid, and violent. Suddenly* RONNIE *has* WILLIE *bent back over an operating table, his hand to his throat, choking him.*)

JENNIFER: The boys are fighting! (*She turns away.*) The boys are fighting again!

WILLIE: No, Ronnie ... don't.

(RONNIE *hesitates for a few moments, then lets go of* WILLIE. WILLIE *gets to his feet. They stand there, staring at each other.* WILLIE *smiles. Suddenly,* RONNIE *turns to the others.*)

RONNIE: Come on! Come on! Get out of it! Get out of it! Willie and Jennifer are leaving.

(*They "snap out of it."*)

BILLINS: Thank God.

ROSE: And are you, are you...

RONNIE: (*Smiling maniacally*) No. I'm staying right here, Mom.

ROSE: Because you're a good boy.

RONNIE: I certainly am.

WILLIE: I forgive you, Ronnie.

(RONNIE *stares at him a long time and then speaks.*)

RONNIE: You were out in the woods, camping with Jennifer. We only wanted to speak to you.

BROWFIELD: Watch it, Ronnie.

RONNIE: I was always on your side, Willie. I was always with you; until one day things just changed. I don't know what it was. But suddenly I was with them, and I was afraid of you.

BROWFIELD: You've said enough, Ronnie.

RONNIE: No one could "control" you. No one could "speak sense" to you. You wouldn't leave us alone. You wouldn't go away.

BROWFIELD: I wash my hands of you, Ronnie.

RONNIE: I was just going to talk to you. It was a cold night. I crossed the shallow part of the river, where all the big yellow stones are. You heard me first, though, and came out of the trees.

WILLIE: Yes.

RONNIE: And then you came down towards me. I didn't know ... what form you were in.

WILLIE: I was myself.

RONNIE: I didn't know. (*Pause*) I waited ... watched you ... walking ... towards me—then you struck me, Willie!

WILLIE: I never moved, Ronnie.

RONNIE: (*Crying out*) Then you struck me, Willie, struck your brother!

BROWFIELD: We saw it, Ronnie! There was moonlight all over the place! He tried to kill you!

WILLIE: I never moved.

RONNIE: And then I stabbed you, Willie! I went crazy and started stabbing you! And then they were on you, Willie, crazier than me, stabbing you to pieces!

ACT TWO

(JENNIFER *cries out and hides her eyes.*)

BROWFIELD: All in self defense, Ronnie. Motivated by the most ironclad reason in eternity.

RONNIE: I wanted nothing to be left of you, Willie. Nothing. (*Pause*) And then I was the last one left holding you ... and I dragged you to where the river was deep and rushing and dropped you there. (*Pause*) And then Jennifer came running out of the tress screaming and trying to get to you but we grabbed her and held her. And then you were gone, Willie, like that like you had never been. Never been.

(*Long silence as* WILLIE *looks at* RONNIE.)

RONNIE: I can't forgive myself, Willie. That's the problem. (*Pause*) For what I've done.

LOU ANN: Don't. Just go with him then. Just leave.

RONNIE: I have to stay here now, Willie. Forever with my loved ones. Forever.

WILLIE: I see, Ronnie.

RONNIE: You understand.

WILLIE: I do. (*He turns to* JENNIFER, *then starts to get his pack. Then he stops and turns to* RONNIE.) Working Boy.

(RONNIE *looks at him for a second, then smiles, realizing what he means.*)

RONNIE: Okay. Sure. (RONNIE *goes to* WILLIE.)

(*The two men begin to sing:*)

> Just a poor working boy,
> Singing the blues,
> Got nothing to gain,
> Got nothing to lose,
> Knocked to the ground
> Bleeding all day,
> Got nothing to love,
> But a half quart of booze.

WILLIE: That's it, man. That's all I've got.

RONNIE: Just a poor working boy!

WILLIE: Sing it, Jack, sing it.

RONNIE: Singing the blues!

WILLIE: Ain't we all, ain't we all.

RONNIE: Got nothing to gain!

WILLIE: Who has? Who has?

RONNIE: Got nothing to lose!

WILLIE: You said it. You know it.

RONNIE: So when they come for my life!

WILLIE: And they will. I know they will.

RONNIE: Tell them to go away!

WILLIE: I sure will. You can count on me.

RONNIE: Because I gave up my life!

WILLIE: I know. I was there.

RONNIE: A long time yesterday!

WILLIE: That's right. You did.

(*Both sing now:*)

> Just a poor working boy,
> Singing the blues,
> Got nothing to gain,
> Got nothing to lose,
> Praying for night...
> But it moves real slow,
> Then suddenly it comes,
> Like a freight through the town,
> And right away it's morning,
> And another go 'round.

WILLIE: And another go 'round.

(*Both men turn toward each other and smile.*)

ACT TWO 75

WILLIE: Good bye, Ronnie.

(*Without anyone seeing him,* WILLIE *has picked up a sharp instrument off the operating table. He now stabs* RONNIE *with it.*)

RONNIE: (*Crying out in shock and pain.*) Willie!

(*Now* WILLIE *stabs him again and* RONNIE *sinks to the floor and dies.*)

LOU ANN: Oh, God, stop it!

BROWFIELD: You did it, Willie, didn't you? You really did it. (*He picks up a sharp instrument from the operating table.*) And now you're going to get it.

(WILLIE, *crying out like an animal, becomes an animal and begins to pursue* BROWFIELD, BILLINS, *and* ROSE *about the room. He begins closing in on* BILLINS.)

BROWFIELD: Watch it, Bijou!

BILLINS: Somebody help me.

(WILLIE *has him cornered, is about to strike, then something comes over him: He begins to slip out of the animal form. He looks about him, somewhat confused;* BILLINS *moves away from him. Now* WILLIE *turns and sees* RONNIE *lying on the ground.* LOU ANN *is holding him in her arms.*)

WILLIE: Oh, Ronnie. Oh, shit, Ronnie. (*He drops the instrument and starts walking toward* RONNIE.)

(*Now* BROWFIELD *suddenly strikes, stabbing* WILLIE *in the back.*)

LOU ANN: No more! No more!

BROWFIELD: (*To* BILLINS *and* ROSE) Help me! Give me a hand! (*He strikes again.*)

(WILLIE *is now lying on the operating table. They all have picked up instruments now and rush to him, stabbing him furiously.*)

(JENNIFER *cries out, falls to the floor, and tries to burrow into the ground.*)

(*They finish stabbing* WILLIE *and stand there, looking at him.*)

BROWFIELD: We had to do it, Bijou. He was a maniac. There was no hope.

ROSE: I'm gonna go talk to Ronnie. (*She starts to go over to* RONNIE.)

BROWFIELD: I think Ronnie's gone, Bijou.

BILLINS: Poor Ronnie.

ROSE: (*To* LOU ANN) Do you mind? Do you mind?

LOU ANN: No, I don't mind at all. (*She gets up.*) But do you mind if I call you Mom?

(ROSE *goes down to* RONNIE. *The men walk over.*)

BROWFIELD: Come on, Bijou, Let's get Ronnie home.

ROSE: That's good, that's good.

(*They lift up* RONNIE *and carry him out.*)

(LOU ANN *paces around a bit, looking at the dogs. Now she turns to* JENNIFER, *who is looking at her.*)

LOU ANN: Some real nice dogs here. (*Pause*) You know what I'm going to do?

JENNIFER: What, Lou Ann?

LOU ANN: I'm gonna let them get Ronnie home and clean him up and patch him up a bit, and then I'm gonna kidnap him.

JENNIFER: Be careful, Lou Ann.

LOU ANN: And take him back to College Town. I mean, we have such good times there. What a dude that Ronnie is! We get so high, we get so turned on by ... by everything ... by life, you know. What a dude that Ronnie is! (*Pause*) You look me up next time you hit College Town, all right?

JENNIFER: I sure will, Lou Ann.

LOU ANN: Day or night, just look me up. (*She exits.*)

ACT TWO

JENNIFER: (*Going to* WILLIE) The boys were fighting again. But it'll be all right. (*Now she begins touching* WILLIE'S *wounds and wiping the blood on her face.*) Because even when Willie sleeps he talks to me, and he gives me things, his dreams, his words, he's watching, because, because he's a good guy—and I love him so.

(*The lights dim and go out.*)

THE END

PROP LIST

ACT ONE
Onstage: 4 lawn chairs
1 small outdoor table

Offstage: 1 lemonade pitcher with lemonade
4 lemonade glasses
1 tea towel
1 handmade "Kill Me" sign (per performance)
1 handmade "Hurt Me Bad" sign (per performance)
1 crash box

Personal: spray breath freshener (BROWFIELD)
pocket toys (BIJOU)

ACT TWO
Onstage: 1 dog with surgical drapery

1 operating table

1 surgical sink

1 small refrigerator

1 wastebasket

2 stools

1 radio

1 six-pack of beer (per performance)

assorted surgical instruments/dressings/supplies

Offstage: stage blood
stage mud
water

Personal: pack of cigarettes (WILLIE)
money in envelope (per performance) (BROWFIELD)

COSTUME PLOT

JENNIFER *ACT ONE*: Cotton shift (denim, faded, very 70's); t-shirt (man's; white, soiled); long underwear (thermal, stained); underpants (boxer shorts); sox (athletic); shoes (high tops—white, dirty); amulet (with assorted talismans and charms); two scarves (remnants from WILLIE); four watches (all broken); rubberbands (several of assorted sizes, worn as bracelets)
  ACT TWO: *Add*—sweater (gray pullover, very large, worn)

BILLINS *ACT ONE*: Pants (navy blue, work); shirt; suspenders; belt (a shoestring); sox; work shoes; handkerchief; jewelry (wedding band)
  ACT TWO: *Add*—tie; raincoat (rubber); rainhat (rubber)

BROWFIELD *ACT ONE*: Pants (brown knit); shirt; jacket (beige twill, Western style); belt (Western, with a fancy buckle); tie; hat; sox; shoes (beige loafers); jewelry (wristwatch; Masonic pin; tiebar; signet ring; diamond pinky ring)
  ACT TWO: *Add*—trenchcoat
    Change to—pajamas; slippers; trenchcoat

ROSE *ACT ONE*: Duster (fussy, with added lace); bib apron; shoes (summer, canvas); pettipants; jewelry (earrings, wedding band, "poodle" pin, wristwatch, crucifix on chain); rosary beads; scapulas (several)
  ACT TWO: Dress (navy, with white dots); shoes (navy flats); sweater (pink, knitted); headscarf (floral); rainbonnet; purse; jewelry (all of above; *add*—sweater guard and pin, a small enamelled rose)

LOU ANN *ACT ONE*: Athletic jersey; underwear (bikini panties, sexy); jewelry (ankle bracelet)

ACT TWO: Dress (cotton knit, very tight); shoes (heels); belt; stockings; jacket (denim, with fleece lining); jewelry (ankle bracelet); *add*—necklace; bracelets; hair ornaments

NOTE: There should be a mud double dress for Lou Ann. On her re-entrance the belt, jewelry, and shoes have been struck.

RONNIE   *ACT ONE*: Jeans (worn, tight); sweatshirt (sleeveless); sneakers; sox; baseball cap

ACT TWO: *Add*—surgeon's smock (bloody); surgeon's cap; rubber gloves; surgical mask

WILLIE   *ACT TWO*: Jacket (extra-long, Army fatigue; back and shoulders of jacket are covered with assorted pieces of animal fur—rabbit, deer, dog, etc.—and stained); overalls (deeply faded and stained); vest (tattered Mexican wool, patterned, torn); shirt (folk shirt, tattered); belt (old, worn, tooled leather, used to keep jacket closed); cap; scarves (several, tattered and shredded; *note*—these should be the same scraps of material that we first see on JENNIFER); boots (old, Western); bag (shoulder, tattered carpetbag)

NOTE: For special make-up, refer to author's description

www.ingramcontent.com/pod-product-compliance
Lightning Source LLC
Chambersburg PA
CBHW071734040426
42446CB00012B/2350